# THE JOY OF THE HARVEST
An Autobiography
**Louis D. Hall**
3084 Hardin Reynolds Rd.
Patrick Springs, VA 24133

# The Joy of the Harvest

Louis D. Hall

Copyright © 2012 by Louis D. Hall
Printed in the USA
Cover design by Beth Hall

## **FORWARD**

Vincent Donovan, missionary to the Maasai tribes in eastern Africa, wrote, *"Evangelization is a process of bringing the gospel to people where they are, not where you would like them to be... When the gospel reaches a people where they are, their response to the gospel is the church in a new place."* For all of my life, for as long as I can remember, my father has been taking the gospel to people where they are in an effort to see the church in new places. I have never known him to have any plan, desire, or ambition to do anything else. It is what he does, and it is who he is.

*The Joy of the Harvest* is more than an autobiography. It is the story of a man who is absolutely convinced that he has good news and feels so compelled to share it that he would make it his life's work.

I am proud of you, Dad, and I love you.

Doug Hall
July 23, 2012
Raleigh, NC

# THE JOY OF THE HARVEST

## Louis D. Hall

This book had its beginning long before I started putting it together a few months ago. It rested in journals, photo albums, notebooks, and scraps of paper in boxes and desk drawers. It was scribbled on backs of revival posters and in church bulletins, across many states and in several foreign nations. It appeared in faded newspaper clippings and in the minds of family members and friends far and wide. For many years I have wanted to pull together all these bits and pieces of my traveling and preaching God's word for more than fifty years and put them in a book. That time has finally arrived and what follows is only a small part of that record. It would be impossible to record all that's happened in these years and now that it's almost complete I think of many things I should have included. I have kept pretty good records thinking I may want to leave this account for my children, grandchildren, and a few friends before I leave this earth. Though I have some memories, there are things that took place in my grandfathers' lives that I'd give the world to know. I was named after both of them. "Louis" from Grandad Craighead who was born in 1867 and "David" from Grandad Hall, born in 1880. No one ever thought about or took the time to write about their lives. Patsy rescued many papers and articles that I had long ago thrown away. As I began to write she produced a large box of them. How blessed I am that she did, as I have them to jog my memory for this book. I encourage everyone reading this to keep a record of your own journey through this life. Someday when you are advanced in years or gone from this world your grandchildren and children and a few friends will thank you for it. I have changed some names and left out some events for fear of offending someone, and may be off in a few places with the dates that certain things took place, but to the best of my memory all of these events happened as I describe them.

In the late 1800's when Dr. David Livingstone wrote about his travels in Africa he said, "I would rather cross the African continent again than undertake to write another book. It is far easier to travel than to write about it." Those are my sentiments exactly, Dr. Livingstone. I make no claim to being an accomplished writer but I do hope that our relationship or friendship will cause the reader to enjoy sharing this journey with me. Since it is not my intention to offer this book for sale, you are reading it as a gift from me or because someone gave you this copy. May you receive as much pleasure reading this as I received in writing it.

Quite often we've heard people say what they would or would not do if they could live their life over. To be perfectly honest, except for some mistakes I've made and people I've hurt or offended, I don't know that I would want to change very much of my life. It's pretty much been about the joy of God's harvest and I wouldn't want to change that. I never became wealthy but I've had enough. Never became famous but then I never cared to. I made plenty of wrong turns and ran into many road blocks, but God always got me turned around and headed in the right direction. I can only thank Him for that.

Thanks to the hundreds of you who have made my life such a full and exciting one, to those who listened to me preach and suffered through my stories and jokes, and to the many who prayed, supported us financially, and encouraged us in this long ministry. I wish I could list all your names. To the many of you who traveled with us to distant lands to share the Gospel, practice dental and medical work, build buildings, teach, and encourage, I thank you. I'm glad you were kept safe and returned home in one piece. To those who worked diligently with us at home in churches throughout the land, I thank you. To the great number of you who obeyed the Gospel under my preaching, both here at home and abroad, I thank God for you. Your names are far too numerous to list. Our God knows who you are and your names are written in Heaven.

A huge thanks goes to my wife, Patsy, and our children Doug, Tammy, and Brenda, and all eight of our grandchildren. If anything good came out of my life and ministry, you were a tremendous part of it. Most people only heard me but you lived with me. Thanks for your love and support.

And last but not least "I thank my God for enabling me and counting me faithful, putting me into the ministry." (1 Tim. 1:12)

## DEDICATION

I lovingly dedicate this book to my wife and very best friend, Patsy. I'm sure I loved you the first time I saw you. Your love, support, and sacrifice along the way has made the difference. It's not been my ministry but our ministry. You have always been willing to go where I felt God was leading and to serve in places that were not always of your choosing. I never heard you complain. Thanks for your willing sacrifice and your love for our dear Lord and for me. I love you.

Louis Hall
May 2012
Patrick Springs, VA

## BEGINNINGS

"It was a dark and stormy night......." Actually it was not. According to my dear Mother, who was there for the occasion, I came into this world on a beautiful but cool September 20 evening in 1935 in the small cotton mill town of Draper in Piedmont North Carolina. Weighing in at about five pounds, I was born in a four room rented company house. Three brothers and a sister were there to welcome me. By the time Dad located old Dr. Ray I was already born. Not that it mattered very much, since the good doctor was a bit tipsy when he arrived anyway. He did manage to fill out a live birth report for my birth certificate and collect a whopping four dollar fee for coming. I smile today when I cross the John B. Ray bridge named for him and wonder how he found his way home that September night. My angel Mother wrapped me in a blanket and welcomed me into her life. Being by far the smallest of the other children she had given birth to she told me when I was older that she feared I may not make it and prayed through the night that God would take care of me. Take care of me He did, and has. By the time I turned sixteen Mom would give birth to four beautiful girls and three boys, bringing the Clyde and Dorothy Hall family to an even dozen.

Growing up in this large family was sheer joy, not to even mention the challenge and adventure. We were a close knit family, and there was never a dull moment in our household. By today's standards we were poor, but most of our friends and school mates in this cotton mill town were in the same condition, so we never thought of ourselves as being poor. This was during the depression, and unemployment hit 25% in 1931. Dad was the only bread winner for our large family and like most every man in town he worked for Marshall Field and Company, later to be called Fieldcrest Mills. He also worked part time at odd jobs to earn some extra money, and the boys hunted and fished as soon as we were old enough. With plenty of wild game and vegetables of a large garden we managed to survive. I can remember being hungry on occasions but Mom could always seem to find something for us to eat. There were plenty of blackberries to pick and Mom canned everything we brought through the door. Owning a cow meant there was always fresh milk and butter, and dad would raise at least two hogs each year. I remember many evenings when supper would be cold milk and hot cornbread. I still enjoy crumbling cornbread in a glass and pouring cold milk over it. It was an exciting time for us when it turned cold enough to kill hogs. The boys were allowed to miss school that day and all the men in the neighborhood helped each other as we went from pen to pen. After the hogs were slaughtered they were placed in a huge trough of boiling water where they were scraped. There was a smell associated with this event that you never forgot. The meat was then cut up and placed in a huge wooden box where it was heavily salted down in order to preserve it. The liver, heart, tenderloin, and sausage were eaten first. Even now I go back to my childhood when I smell sausage frying. For whatever reason someone usually saved the pig tail, tied a red ribbon on it, and gave it to someone for Christmas.

    Dad usually managed to have a few toys for us at Christmas but most of the things we played with were homemade. Slingshots were made from a forked branch of a small bush or tree and two strips of rubber cut from an inner tube with a small leather pad (the tongue from an old shoe worked great) to hold the stone. Few boys were ever without a slingshot. Hide and seek was a favorite game and sometimes a boy would sneak off home and go to bed when they hid. The person who was "IT" might look for them an hour or more. One of the more dangerous games we played was to make a ball about the size of a baseball out of string, soak it a good while in kerosene, set it on fire, and play catch. Obviously no one held the ball very long. A favorite game of mine was to stand under a street light and toss small stones in the air. When a bat would fly at them we'd swing at them with long sticks. I don't recall ever hitting one of these radar-equipped creatures. All of these games were always played at night. Shooting marbles was a great summer game, and boys jeans pockets would be bulging with these beautiful objects. The alley ball or "beauty" as we called it was the shooter marble and was always larger than the others. Sometimes we'd use a ball bearing to shoot with. The object was to knock as many as you could out of a circle. The shooter got to keep what he knocked out.

Within sight of our house at the edge of the pasture was a large hickory tree. We all referred to it as "The Big Tree." What a wonderful place to retreat to! It provided shade over a large area on the hot summer days, and its limbs were wonderful to climb on. At age eleven two thrilling things happened to me high up in that old tree. The first was that I became a bombardier aboard a B-52 dropping bombs over Germany. I would carry sacks of rocks onto those high limbs and drop them on imaginary targets below. The second thing was the realization that I was madly in love. I met her in fourth grade. Her name was Barbara Stultz, and I knew she loved me since she gave me a store-bought valentine card that year. It didn't matter that she gave everyone else in the class one also. My card had said, "Be My Valentine." What? She wanted me to be her valentine? I sure would! The thing that made me realize I loved her was the day I climbed to the top of that tree, pulled out my Barlow pocket knife, and carved our initials high in "The Big Tree." I would sit for long periods of time and dream of her welcoming me as I came home from across the sea, a war hero. Or weeping loudly over my flag-draped casket after my plane was shot down in the South China Sea. I was sure the day would come when we would marry.

A few weeks ago I was having coffee in a little restaurant in my hometown when a man approached and said, "Louis?" It was Barbara's older brother, Otis. I had not seen him in 60 years. We enjoyed talking about old times but I never asked about his sister. I didn't want to know. I long ago concluded that she was living the life of a lonely old maid or that she converted from Baptist to Catholic and has lived in a convent all these years. I only hope that Otis doesn't tell his sister he saw me looking so well and happy. She's suffered enough and I wouldn't want to add to her pain.

Few boys in Draper were ever without a stick. When you

found your favorite stick it just became a part of you. It was good for walking and for warding off barking dogs. It could easily change a bully's mind and worked well for me when I was confronted by bully Tommy Howell. It was great for poking around in someone's trash can and splashing water from a mud hole. What better way to handle a snake than with a stick? How convenient they were when playing "Cowboys and Indians." You could carefully swing it between your legs and ride off into the sunset. Or you could just as easily use it as a guitar as you sang, "Happy trails to you until we meet again....." There were a few other games we played with sticks that I'd best not write about. It could be that the statute of limitations has not yet run out.

    I'm thinking lately that maybe it would be good to put the sticks back on active duty . It would get the kids out in the fresh air. Sticks are far less expensive than video games, computers, and iPods. There are no costly repairs when one breaks, and they are easily replaced. They would eliminate the big problem we're having with bullying and establish confidence in the boy who carries one. They are fairly safe since no one ever got shot with a stick. Sticks are far better for one's health (unless you're a bully) than sitting in front of the TV eating potato chips and drinking pop. During the years that we did missionary work in Haiti the country was constantly in turmoil. I cut a stick from a piece of two by four, carved the words "Lou's Ugly Stick" on the side, and filled in the letters with red paint. I carried it with me in the truck wherever I went. Thankfully I never had to use it, but there were several occasions when it earned me a lot of respect and discouraged a few would be bullies. Anyway, I have always appreciated Exodus 4:2 in which God said to Moses, "'What is that in your hand?' And he said, 'A stick.'" It's hard to beat being in the company of men like Moses.

    Sometime in the summer of 1948 I was playing marbles with my friend Nelson in the front yard of our home place, when my brother Carl pulled up in his car. Out of the trunk of his Kaiser car he lifted a beautiful green bicycle. It had a battery operated horn and light and whitewall tires. It had a luggage rack on the back. I had never seen anything so beautiful, and then Carl said, "See if it fits you." It was the first and only bicycle I ever owned, and it brought me more hours of enjoyment that I could ever describe. I still look up to this older brother and think of his kindness to a young brother so very often. I've had many motorcycles since that day and am the owner of a Honda Goldwing motorcycle as I write this, but I've never had a ride that meant as much to me as the green Firestone bike.

On September 2, 1940, 18 days before my 6$^{th}$ birthday, I was taken to school by my oldest sister, Helen. She left me in Mrs. Thompson's first grade class at the old Draper Graded school. I was extremely shy and slipped out the door and ran home after about thirty minutes. I never liked school from the first day and learned all about skipping even in the first grade. I missed so many days in grade one that I had to repeat it the next year. Dad would often take me to school in his '37 Chevy and I would beat him back home. One of my favorite tricks was to leave the school grounds as soon as the bell rang and hang out in an old barn until school was over for the day. I would spend the day playing alone in this large shed and hiding in the hay loft. This was a year before America's involvement in World War 2, but talk of war was in the air and I delighted to play soldier in Ben Moore's old shed. I would have been quite an excited boy had I known that one day I would be a real soldier in the U.S. Army, have my Pilot's Certification and own and fly my own airplane.

Though I was not even seven years old yet, I vividly remember Dad calling us to the house and making us sit quietly in front of a Farnsworth floor model radio (which I have today, thanks to my brother Carl.) Edward R. Murrow was speaking and gave us the news that Japan had bombed Pearl Harbor. I remember President Roosevelt trying to assure the nation not to fear. America was now at war. It was December 7, 1941. I was six years old but I well remember the day.

Great numbers of men from this small town were quick to volunteer for action. Some of them died in these far away places, and streets are named for them in my hometown. My oldest brother, Carl, was 16 at the time but in two years he would be a gunner and crew member aboard a PBY somewhere in the South Pacific. The PBY was a search and rescue aircraft and played a huge part in the war effort. Their job was to search for downed airmen and pluck them from the waters of the South Pacific. Carl's letters home were censored as were all those serving, but he and Mom worked out a code whereby he could keep us informed of his whereabouts. There was a large board erected in Draper with the names of all who were serving. Throughout the war I would stand with pride as I passed and read his name. It would be almost two years before he would be home again. There was a spirit of patriotism during this time that brings tears to my eyes to remember. Five of us Hall boys would serve tours in the military in the years to come and all would return home safely because of our Mom's prayers. By the time this war was over I would be ten years old and could name Generals like Patton, MacArthur, and "Ike" Eisenhower.

My dislike for school continued until I reached the 5$^{th}$ grade and met a teacher that turned my life around. Mrs. Edwards was a small, soft-spoken lady in her 40's. I can't ever recall her raising her voice when she spoke to us. She was wise enough to know who did and who didn't like school and which of her students were trying. One day she asked me to stay a few minutes after school so she could talk with me. I believe to this day she saw the wandering fever in me and knew that I longed to see what lay beyond the little town I lived in. Though it's been more than 60 years, I recall her sitting in a school desk next to me with several books in her hands. She began by saying, "Louis, you love adventure, don't you?" I assured her I did, and she continued, "If you would learn to read well, you could travel all over the world in books." She went on to speak of Columbus and his search for new lands, and of Lindbergh and his solo flight across the Atlantic. She showed me pictures of the great Taj Mahal in India. I thought of her when I saw it for the first time in 1972. When Patsy and I first saw Niagara Falls, the Grand Canyon, and the Alps I laughed and said, "Mrs. Edwards told me about these." When school was out that summer I went to the library at the YMCA and got a library card. I read at least two books each week until school began again that fall. This gentle woman never knew what she did for me. She planted a love for books in my heart that has only grown through the years. Even at my advanced age I average reading two or three books each week. How could I have ever known that I would one day travel around the world several times and visit and preach in exotic and interesting places I had only read about? Mrs. Edwards only whetted my appetite to see and experience what lay beyond my small hometown.

The remaining seven years of my local schooling were rather uneventful. I was never a straight "A" student but managed to pass each grade without difficulty. I took Machine Shop in High School and learned how to weld and run a lathe and milling machine. I had neither the dream, desire, nor the money to attend college, so I guessed I would be a machinist or work in the cotton mill. As I think back on it after all these years I don't ever remember anyone encouraging me to go to college.

On Saturdays, Sundays, and daily during the summers I worked as a caddy at Meadow Greens Country Club, a nine hole golf course located a few miles from home. On a good day I could make $1.20 for the entire day. That included 70 cents from the Club and 50 cents tip from the golfer. The tip was not a sure thing and would often be a quarter or even a dime. On February 23, 1946 while I was caddying a golfer hit a low hook that caught me above my left ear. I was taken to the old Leaksville Hospital where I lay unconscious for almost a week. I missed twenty one days of school. The Country Club gave me a check for $21.00 - a dollar per day for every day I was unable to caddy. I was ten years old and this was by far the greatest amount of money I had ever had. Within an hour of hearing the news that I was hurt Mom got the news that her Mother had died about the same hour in Roanoke, Virginia. Out of her great concern for me she never made the trip for Grandma Craighead's funeral. Mom loved her saintly Mother and her ten year old boy dearly so this had to be a day of grief and weeping for my precious Mother.

I cut grass with a push mower for 50 cents, regardless the size of the yard. In the winter I set up pins at the YMCA bowling alley for 10 cents a frame. On a good Saturday I could set up about 30 frames and make $3 plus tips. That was good money then, but I worked from 10 AM until 9 PM. After the YMCA closed at 9 PM I would often go to the Draper Café where I would order a hamburger steak. It was a large piece of hamburger covered with gravy and included fries and a hot roll. Washed down with a cold bottled Pepsi or Double Cola, it cost me a whopping 35 cents of that hard earned money.

One really hilarious incident with regards to working happened when I was about thirteen years old. A schoolmate came to me and asked if I wanted to join him in a venture that would pay us good money with almost no work. Of course the "good money" and "almost no work" parts interested me, but when he told me we would have to be very careful and secretive about it and that it was kind of like being in the FBI I was even more intrigued. It turned out that one of our schoolteachers and my friend's neighbor was convinced that her husband was seeing another woman. She had given my friend a couple of dollars and asked him to go to her husband's place of business, observe him from time to time, and report back to her what he saw. He would give me half of what she gave him if I would join him as a spy. It all sounded pretty good to me. There was no hard work involved in this. I never gave broken bones and bleeding body parts a thought. I really laugh now when I remember how we envisioned this "spy business" growing. There were all kind of rumors of things going on in the little town of Draper. Everyone had heard stories of the police getting payoffs from bootleggers, and it was well known that a taxi company in town would bring a pint of whiskey whenever you called. (I knew because that's how my uncle got his.) Once when walking home late at night I saw a young doctor come out of the boarding house where another young schoolteacher of mine lived. They stood on the porch and kissed. Someone might want to know that. Of course they later married, so if we had sold that information we might have had to give them a refund. I was all over that small town as a boy and saw all kinds of things that people might pay good money to know. I collected coupons from cans and boxes to redeem for a pocket watch or knife so I knew what was in trash cans all around town. We thought some preachers would be willing to pay to know what we saw in some of their members cans, or maybe in the minister's cans. If we began digging there was no telling what we might find. There would be enough work to last a long time. Anyway, we had been in the spy business about two weeks when I went into his place of business just to look around. He approached me smiling and suddenly grabbed me by the shirt collar and said, "What are you doing spying on me? Do you want me to break your back?" I was so terrified, I replied, "No Ma'am." I ended my career as a spy that very day.

At age fifteen and sixteen I played football with the Draper YMCA. There was a shortage of players so most of us played both offense and defense. I played left guard. It was a well equipped team and coached by Vance Reese who had played football at Draper High and Elon College. This team, the Bantams, played throughout North Carolina and my first year we went 9-1. The last game of the year was played on Thanksgiving day at Schoolfield, VA. This was an all black team, which was unusual during the days of strict segregation. They devastated us to the tune of 52-0. They knocked us all over the field and when the game was finally over they wanted to fight us with their fists. I don't remember that we ever advanced beyond our own 30 yard line. Each time the ball was snapped the big guy opposite me would spit on me and send me flying.

Toward the end of the game, our quarterback, Ken McCray called huddle, and rather than give us the play, he said in desperation, "Everybody just do something." These were supposed to be 15 and 16 year olds, but on our way home fullback Jerry Bateman remarked, "That's the first time I was ever tackled by a guy with a beard and gray hair." Coach Reese said, "I saw his son on the sideline cheering for him."

At the close of that winning season we had a banquet, and the all-American football player from University of North

Carolina, Charlie (Choo Choo) Justice was the speaker.

One tremendous advantage of being a caddie at the golf course was that caddies were allowed to play on Monday. This was free, and the golfers would loan their caddies their clubs. Some of us became pretty good golfers. About this time black boys were beginning to show up to caddie. One such young man was a tall, athletic-looking kid named Joe Artis. Evidently no golfer would loan their clubs to him so he used what he had. I can testify truthfully to what follows because I was there the day it happened. Joe took a broken 3-iron he had found and taped it back together. He had an old beat-up 8-iron, and he cut a root out of the woods and whittled it down into a putter. On a beautiful summer day he shot a 35 at the old Meadow Greens Country Club. This was one over par 34. I often wonder what this young man could have done had he been living today. Maybe another Tiger Woods.

In 1951 four of us from the football team and a girl named Pat Coleman organized a bowling team at the YMCA. We called ourselves the "KILLROYS" and would bowl against adult teams in a league. We won the championship that year and at the banquet we looked forward to those large trophies given out every year. To our great surprise we were given marble-size bowling balls to wear on a key chain. Bummer. At least the food at the banquet was good.

This is a good place to share a little of what the Draper YMCA meant to me and so many other boys in this small town. It cost fifty cents to belong, but if you couldn't pay that you could still come to the "Y" as we called it. It was a large building and a warm retreat on a cold day. In the summer there was a large front porch with chairs. It was a place where all your friends gathered and you could go there even if you didn't have a dime. I saw my first television here and also took my very first shower. I can still smell the Lifebuoy soap. Neither could I ever forget that it was in the reading room of the library which adjoined the "Y" that at the age of 14 I finally kissed a girl. She wasn't a sweetheart or girlfriend, and I can't recall how it came about, but I do remember I wasn't very good at it. I'll never know why I waited until I was an old man to do this. I do remember thinking this was something I could come to like. And I have.

I'm firmly convinced that this old Draper "Y" kept many a Draper boy out of trouble and maybe out of prison or worse. Funny how it was one of the first places you visited when you came home on leave from the military. Many of us thought about it when we were far away and lonesome for home. I owe a great debt of thanks to those who have gone on who kept those doors open for me.

When I was 17 I went to work at the golf course as the greens keeper's helper making $15 per week. When the head greens keeper quit a few months later, I got his job making $30.00 per week consisting of five and a half days. I loved the job and couldn't wait to get to work each day and climb on that Toro tractor. I took great pride in my work and was always pleased when told that Meadow Greens Country Club had the prettiest greens in the area. Once when management from the prestigious Sedgefield County Club out of Greensboro came to look at our greens I didn't reveal to them that I had often brought my date to the course at 10 PM some nights and had her help me put the sprinklers on and let them water the greens until I went to work at 7 AM. Neither did I tell them I had given the caddies fifteen cents for each bucket of crab grass they cut out of the greens. When asked the secret to such beautiful greens, I humbly said, "Just hard work, I guess. I really don't know."

I graduated from Tri-City High School in June 1954. I had no earthly idea what I would do or even what I could do, and I continued to work at the golf course through the summer.

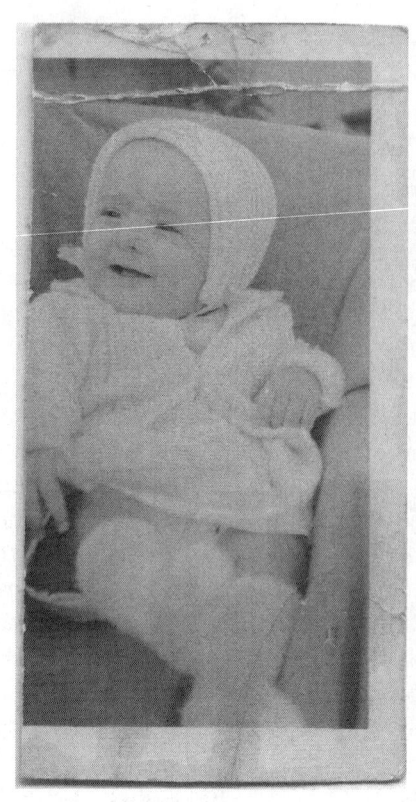

Above: Louis, early 1936

Top right: Louis, mid 1940s

Right: Louis, early 1940s

## YOU'RE IN THE ARMY NOW

     A good paying job was difficult to find in the fall of 1954, especially if you were draft age. So when some of my friends began leaving for college and others began enlisting in the military I knew I had to do something. I hitchhiked to the local draft board in Reidsville, NC and asked them to draft me into the United States Army. I remember stopping at my sister Helen's house that day, and when I told her what I'd done she hugged me and cried. She was my oldest sister and always loved me dearly. I loved her and her sweet spirit. I sat at her table that day and ate cornbread and beans. She promised to write me when I was in the Army and she did. I could have joined, but my obligation would be three years. If I was drafted I would only have a two year hitch, and the G.I. benefits were the same. Within a month I received my notice to report for induction at Charlotte, NC. I had just turned nineteen. My plan was to leave before daylight that October 25th morning and not wake anyone in the house, thus eliminating any sad goodbyes. Mom always cried when her boys left for military service. But as I dressed to leave I could smell bacon frying, and slipping into the kitchen I saw Mom preparing breakfast on an old wood stove she cooked on for years. As her tears fell on her apron she served me bacon and eggs with her famous hot biscuits and Karo syrup. She didn't eat. I choked it down as I choked back my own tears. I had no idea how long I would be gone and if I would ever see home again. I kissed this precious little woman goodbye and she spoke five words, "Louis, remember who you are." I knew what she meant by that. I had just become a Christian and she knew the temptations in the military would be great and she wanted me to remember that I now belonged to the Lord Jesus Christ. I never forgot that and haven't forgotten it to this very day. It was the best advice a Mother could have ever given a son.

## FORT JACKSON, SOUTH CAROLINA

I had been told by the draft board that after my examination in Charlotte I would be allowed to return home and given two weeks to get my business in order before reporting for duty. I had told my new girlfriend we would take in a movie on Saturday night. After passing the physical, which included the strange command to pee in a bottle, I raised my right hand and took one step forward and I now belonged to Uncle Sam. We were all promptly herded onto olive drab buses and sent on our way to Fort Jackson, SC. I guess it really didn't matter since I had no business to put in order anyway. I spent the first eight weeks with the 101$^{st}$ Airborne Division at Fort Jackson, SC. The 101$^{st}$ was and is one of the most prestigious outfits in the U.S. Army. During World War 2 it fought at Normandy and also the battle of the Bulge. It saw action in Korea, Vietnam, Iraq and Afghanistan. I was proud to wear the shoulder patch with The Screaming Eagle. Life in basic training was rigid and demanding but not unbearable. I was accustomed to waking early, and unlike most, I found the food to be pretty good. The infamous S.O.S. was not my favorite but I ate it. I learned to eat food that I had never tried before. The days and nights passed quickly due to the schedule we kept. We drilled and sat in class six full days per week. On Sunday morning we could march to the chapel on post. Since I was a new Christian I greatly enjoyed this and looked forward to it every week. We attended protestant services and I don't recall ever hearing a message that inspired me, but the singing was wonderful and gave me an opportunity to express my faith. Anyway, no one screamed at you or got in your face in chapel. I could even catch a few winks of much needed sleep. Sunday afternoons were spent cleaning gear and getting ready to begin again on Monday. After a few weeks of physical training we began making those five mile marches with fifty pound packs. We joked that on beautiful days they hauled us out to the rifle range in covered trucks, but on rainy days they marched us there. I had been shooting a gun since I was a small boy so the rifle range was a welcome sight. After a week of qualifying, I fired Expert with the M1. I recall the Range Sergeant asking if I would be interested in sniper school. I declined!

Ask anyone who was ever in the military and they will tell you what a special time mail call was. Mom and my girlfriend wrote often and this really helped ease the times of loneliness. Our only problem was that we had a mail clerk who liked to play games with our mail. He would always read the return address aloud and Heaven forbid if there was anything written on the back of the envelope or if it had the slightest smell of perfume or trace of lipstick. His favorite trick was to write down the return address and say, "I think I'll write this girl." Or he might say, "I'll give you this letter when you give me ten pushups." He was a short, skinny guy with an ego bigger than a barn and barely more rank than we had. On the day we graduated four of us went looking for him, but he couldn't be found at Fort Jackson.

I walked guard duty on Christmas day and graduated from basic training on December 27. About 70 of us left the next day for Camp Gordon, GA where I would undergo advanced infantry training with the $2^{nd}$ Infantry Division. Its primary mission was then and is today the defense of South Korea. In 1954 the division consisted of 27,000 troops. My outfit, Company "H", had 176 battle-ready soldiers. I still remember the definition learned in a class on military strategy as being: "The maneuvering of troops and weapons to the best advantage in meeting the enemy."

I made some great friends at Camp Gordon. One of them, Pfc. Evans from Macon, GA would often say, "Hall, we don't make much money but we sure have a lot of fun." My first month's pay as a Private was exactly $87.50. That was $32.50 less than I made as head greens keeper back home. Perhaps some of that was due to a statement made by my Commander-in-chief President "Ike" Eisenhower, himself a military man, when he said, "All the soldier needs is pocket change." That's about all we had.

While in the field at Camp Gordon we lived in two-man pup tents. One dark night PFC Evans and I decided if we were really careful we could get away with having a smoke inside the tent we shared. This was during war games we were participating in and there was to be no light anywhere. We lit our cigarettes and did our best to shield them with our steel helmets. After only a few puffs our tent was suddenly uprooted from around us. Standing above us was Master Sgt Flood. He was about six foot three inches tall and weighed about 230 pounds. We spent the rest of the night digging a four foot hole to bury the cigarette butts in. This wasn't the last time those Lucky Strikes would get me in trouble before I wised up and quit them.

    In early February we had finished this phase of our training and I received orders stamped "Pipeline." All I knew was that I would be going somewhere in the far east. I was given a fifteen day leave and was to report to Fort Totten, NY after that. I would find out where my new duty station was at that time. From Camp Gordon I took a bus to the train station in Augusta and purchased a ticket to Danville, VA for $10.75. As I stood on the platform waiting for the train I heard a peppy song by the Chordettes entitled "Mister Sandman." This song would be number one on the charts and became a favorite of mine. I can listen to it now on YouTube and it takes me back 57 years to a train station in Georgia and a nineteen year old soldier in uniform who was so happy to be going home again. If you don't know this song, take a break from the book right now and listen to it on YouTube. Close your eyes and picture this young soldier standing on a train platform in late afternoon during a cold drizzle, happy to be heading home.

    It was great to be home again and with family. Hunting season was in and I greatly enjoyed hunting rabbit and quail with a great brother, Kenneth. My sweet Mom thought I was starving and filled me with her hot biscuits, milk gravy, mashed potatoes, and Bunker Hill beef. Her chocolate pie would melt in your mouth and no one baked an egg custard pie like Mom Hall. It was more than wonderful to see the change in my Dad since he had given his life to Christ. We were not a church going family and all of my life up till now Dad had a serious problem with alcohol. There would be periods of time when he would quit drinking but later he would take it up again. It never kept him from working and he had always provided for his family but the booze was costly to him and the entire family in so very many ways. Now that he was a Christian he had quit drinking for good. Dad never drank alcohol again after that. He had been baptized while still wearing a cast after an auto accident in which several family members were seriously injured. Now I marveled as I observed him reading the Bible and attending church on a regular basis. My brother Russell, who had recently completed a tour in the Air Force, returned home and became a Christian. He was now at Cincinnati Bible Seminary in Ohio, studying for the ministry. God was working mightily in our family but at this time I had no idea what He had in mind and how this would include me. I liked military life and as far as I was concerned this would be as good a career as any. Little did I know that I would live to be an "Old Soldier" but not for Uncle Sam.

On February 19, 1955 I caught the Southern Crescent train in Danville, VA for New York City. When I disembarked at Grand Central station, carrying my duffel bag with everything I owned in it, I was totally lost. I had never seen so many people and all in a hurry to get somewhere. When I spied a wiener stand, I asked for a hot dog, all the way. In broken English the vendor said, "All the way? All the way? I don't know your all the way." With that, he slapped a wiener in a bun and handed it to me. If I wanted mustard and relish, I got it myself. My first taste of a Yankee hot dog was sure not like the good ol' Southern hot dogs I had enjoyed at the Knotty Pine in Draper. I promptly got on the wrong subway train and wound up at Brooklyn Navy Yard which was definitely not where a soldier needed to be. After several failed attempts I found Fort Totten. It was located near Bayside in Queens, NY. It was then headquarters for the 41$^{st}$ Anti-Aircraft Gun Battalion. Upon reporting I learned my orders had been changed and I was to report to "C" Battery 41st AAA Gun Battalion. This was the beginning of the Cold war and eight batteries of five large 90mm anti-aircraft guns had been set strategically around NYC to guard it from enemy attack. These were the days when attack from Russia was fully expected and we watched the skies around the clock. How could I have ever guessed that the attack would not come from Russia and during my watch but from Muslim extremists and 46 years later?

My first duty with the 41$^{st}$ was radar operator, definitely not what I had trained for but it kept me out of the cold NY weather as I watched the 'scope in the radar room. "C" battery was manned by about 60 men so friendships were made quickly.We lived in small huts with about 20 men each and worked a pretty normal eight hour shift. I still had to pull guard duty and K.P. on a fairly regular basis, so when the Company Commander, Captain Forteau called me to his office and asked if I would be interested in being his private driver, I jumped at the chance. This would mean no more guard duty or K.P., and when not driving the "Old man" around I would clean the Jeep and have it ready. I was assigned to the Motor Pool and sometimes drove the "Five Tons" as they were called, to transfer troops or ammunition to other sites.

Every few months we would pull these huge guns across Long Island to Montauk Point where we would fire them at targets out on the ocean for about a week. Once during our practice firing a shell exploded killing two of the guys on the gun. I was handling ammunition at the time and felt a little sting to my left leg. It never gave me any trouble. More than 40 years later a piece of the shrapnel worked itself out while I was in the shower. I showed it to Patsy and thought about what might have been. I'll always believe the unseen hand of God was on me, protecting me for a job He had for me on down the road.

My brother Russell wrote to me from Bible College and told me about a girl who had recently dropped out of college and moved back to New York. He encouraged me to go see her. I'm sure he thought this would influence my interest in church and since he had spent four years in the Air Force he knew what temptations we faced daily. Having the captain's Jeep at my disposal, I drove the twenty miles to her house in Brooklyn and met her and her mother. Her dad had been one of four men who died while building the Empire State Building. She was not the most beautiful girl I'd ever dated but as Barney Fife told Gomer, "She was nice." I enjoyed her company and she invited me to Hicksville Church of Christ out on Long Island where she was a member. After a few dates and visits to church, she suddenly broke it off. When I pressed her to give me a reason she finally said her minister had smelled cigarette smoke on me and warned her not to get serious about a GI. He assured her I would lead her astray and, like all soldiers, I was only looking for a good time. I never saw her again and never heard anymore about her. I did wonder what would have been wrong with having a good time. I was far away from home, lonely, and we did have a good time together. Forty-eight years later in 2003 I met her preacher again when I was invited to speak at Roanoke Bible College's Gospel Rally. He was the song leader. At lunch I asked him if he remembered a Muriel Chamberlain from Brooklyn. I had to smile when he said, "Oh yes, she was a nice girl." I then asked if he remembered a young soldier bringing her to church in an Army Jeep. He couldn't recall the event, so I dropped it. When I got up to put away my tray, I did whisper to him, "By the way, I quit smoking many years ago." I have no idea if he ever figured it all out, but just think, if not for the cigarettes and Army uniform I might have married a "Nice Yankee" from Brooklyn rather than a beautiful girl from Ohio. Thank God, Uncle Sam, and Lucky Strikes.

    New York was an exciting and interesting place to live and I often went to the U.S.O. for free movie tickets and Broadway shows. I could attend N.Y. Yankee games for free through the U.S.O. I would spend nineteen months watching the skies of New York and driving our company commander wherever he needed to go. It wasn't a bad job but I still knew something was missing. There was something I needed to be doing but I had no idea what it was. I had been told that when I went into the Army I would forget all about God but that did not happen. If anything, I thought about Him more and more and wanted to serve Him. I just didn't know how that could be. Though none of my fellow soldiers did this, I made Bible study a daily thing. On days like Thanksgiving and Christmas the Captain would ask me to give thanks for our meal. I picked up the nickname "Preacher" though I had no intention of ever doing that. Throughout my entire life I had done everything within my power to avoid speaking to a group large or small and could not imagine ever doing that. Unless I was with someone I really knew and liked, I was introverted. I had grown up with the idea that I didn't measure up to others. I had an inferiority complex. Even today there are times when I have to remind myself that God made me in His own image and gave me life. Maybe someone reading this book needs the reminder that God has a plan for your life. You and I are of great value to Him. So much so that He sent His dear Son to die for us.

In early October 1956 Captain Forteau again called me to his office and gave me the pep talk for re-enlistment. The Army was offering me my next stripe and a $500 bonus if I extended for another year. He explained that I could retire at age 39. I thanked him and kindly declined the offer. I was proud and happy that I had made the decision to serve my country. I still am. It was the right thing for me to do. Two years of my life was a small price to pay for what America had given to me. The defense of our country was probably stronger in 1956 than it had ever been before. I had no idea what would follow my military life, but I would go back home to North Carolina and maybe God would show me. I had not lost my faith as some predicted. It was stronger than when I left home.

On October 26, 1956 I received a separation from the U.S. Army, processing out at Fort Dix, NJ. I had served two years and one day and would receive my discharge in six years. I would be in the reserves for the next six years and was in fact called up again during the Cuban Missile Crisis in October 1962 when the Soviet Union and the United States squared off over the placement of Soviet missiles in Cuba just 90 miles from the United States. My active and inactive time was up a week later and so I wasn't required to report.

I took my time coming home from New York, taking

about three days to get home. I stopped in Philadelphia and Washington and took in some sights that I had always wanted to see. I remember a restlessness stirring in me that I just couldn't understand. I couldn't shake the feeling that I should be planning for something but I had no idea what it was.

Right: U.S. Army, 1956

Below: P.F.C. Hall, 1955

## BACK TO CIVILIAN LIFE

I was surprised to find that I didn't miss the disciplined life of the Army, and for a few weeks I enjoyed being free to hunt and fish and sleep in if I so desired. Mom hadn't lost a thing in her cooking and the fellowship with Dad and other siblings was sheer joy. Dad was an avid bass fisherman, and we greatly enjoyed climbing over the rocks on Smith river as he looked for that big one that got away in the summer. Those memories bring tears to my eyes as I record them now. I was past twenty-one and it was surely time to go to work, but where? I faced the same problem I had prior to the military - there were very few jobs available. I worked as a land surveyor's helper, pulling chain and clearing brush. We surveyed many miles of land in and around Cascade and Brosville, VA. The owner of the company even offered to send me to Georgia Tech to study Engineering in exchange for my working for the company for five years, but I had no interest. I worked for Adams Electric Company in Cleveland, TN for about five months. My job was installing light fixtures and pulling wire in a new textile plant being built. When workers went on strike and began picketing the plant things began to get rough. I told my brother-in-law who worked there, "If I wanted to fight I would have stayed in the Army." I turned in my hard hat and tools and hitchhiked back home. There I worked at a lumber company unloading boxcars and loading finished lumber into trucks for delivery. I made minimum wage which was $1.00 per hour. After taxes, etc. I brought home about $33.00 for 40 hours which was $3.00 more than I made at the golf course in 1953-54. I felt no fulfillment nor saw any future in this. From November 1956 until August 1957 I worked at all these jobs without any feeling of accomplishment or joy. I was approaching twenty-two years of age and had no car and no savings, was still living at home, and had no idea what it was I should be doing. I had talked with an Army recruiter and was considering re-enlisting when it happened...

During my last few months in the military, one of the saddest events of my life took place. The church where I had given my life to Christ experienced a split. A fairly large number, including my own family, left the church to establish a new work in town. Various reasons for the split were given, all depending on which side you talked with. As I look back on it fifty years later there was plenty of blame to be given both sides. It was a split that never should have taken place. As is usually the case in church fights, it had to do with power and who would be in charge. I long ago concluded that the vast majority of church splits could easily be avoided if people would just love each other and sit down to talk over their differences. I was caught in the middle. My family wanted me to attend the new work at Lincoln Street (later Central) Church of Christ) but my heart was at Draper Christian. I loved those people and never did understand why the church divided. I tried to solve the problem by attending both. How could I have ever dreamed that in fifteen years I would be called as minister of Draper Christian church and have one of my best ministries there? I still love them dearly and they love me. I have family members and dear friends there today. It was sometime in May while attending worship at Draper that I heard a message preached entitled "What Will You Do?" "What will you do with Jesus? What will you do with your Bible? What will you do with your neighbor? *What will you do with the rest of your life?*" I had not thought much about that last question but now I began to. Was it even possible that I might be able to preach? It sure seemed far-fetched. Russell was now a junior at Cincinnati Bible Seminary (now Cincinnati Christian University) and was already preaching in West Virginia. He was constantly encouraging me to join him in College, and Dad, an elder by now, was praying and encouraging me also. So in early June I applied and was accepted as a freshman student. I smile now when I remember one of the questions on the application, "Do you use tobacco?" I took them out of my shirt pocket and tossed them in the trash and answered the question, "No." Those cigarettes had already cost me a "Nice Yankee Girl". I wouldn't let them keep me out of Bible College. I never smoked another cigarette after that. On August 24, 1957 Dad took me to Martinsville, VA and I hitchhiked to Cincinnati, OH. My life was about to change and I would soon discover what it was God wanted of me.

## HEAVEN ON EARTH

I absolutely loved Bible college life from day one. The campus was situated on Price Hill, overlooking the city of Cincinnati, a bustling and friendly city with plenty of jobs for students and plenty of fun things to do. Longfellow had dubbed it the "Queen of the West." I fell in love with the Queen City immediately and to this day it remains a favorite place for us to retreat for vacation and rest. One of the favorite foods of the city is Skyline Chili. It consisted of thin spaghetti with chili, cheese, and onions on top and was a favorite of most of the students on campus. Fortunately for me Patsy discovered the recipe years later and makes it often for us.

Life on campus was unlike anything I had ever experienced. The students were outgoing and friendly and friendships were made that have endured all my life. I saw a deep joy in them that I had never seen anywhere else. They really loved the Lord and were not ashamed to say so. There seemed to always be a group gathered around a piano somewhere, singing praises to God. The Bible was seldom out of sight and prayer groups were common. With this type of influence I felt myself growing in the grace and knowledge of Christ. I was truly the happiest I had ever been and was starting to think God had something exciting and worthwhile in store for me. I still could not think of myself a preacher but I was enjoying this new-found joy. Fairly early in my freshman year I met a blue eyed, Scotch-Irish girl on campus named Patsy McBee. I remember thinking she was the most beautiful girl I had ever seen and wanted to ask her out, but guessed I would have little chance with this lovely lady. I told my roommate, "She is five foot two with eyes that are bluer and prettier than the North Carolina skies." When I told her that her eyes were "Carolina Blue", she smiled and blushed slightly. The wheels turned in my head when she revealed her desire to be a missionary and was, in fact, working in a downtown mission at that time. I didn't know it, but God was getting ready to do something in my life that I couldn't have done in a million years. Other than saving my soul, Patsy would be the best thing to happen to me for the rest of my life. I was definitely not a ladies man and dated only one other girl in my freshman year. She was Greta Bradfield from Dayton, OH. Greta was a tall, pretty girl with beautiful brown eyes and long hair. She loved the Lord with all her heart. But as Johnny Cash sang,

> "I never got over those blue eyes -
> I see them every where."

Classes were held Tuesday thru Friday from 7:00AM until noon. I worked for the J.C. Penney Co. From 1 PM until 5 PM. Evenings were filled with study. I wasn't an "A" student but never failed a course in the entire four years of college. I especially enjoyed the Bible courses taught by godly men who had studied the Bible most of their lives. My two favorite courses were Acts and The Life of Christ. Even today I find the majority of my messages coming from these books. As I sat in class each day I had no idea that I studied with students who would go to the ends of the earth as missionaries and preachers of the Gospel. Some would even die in these far away places. Others would fill pulpits in great churches throughout our country and serve as faculty members in our bible colleges. Many of my fellow students were "spiritual giants" in the making and I didn't know it. My first roommate was Fred Schreiber from Indiana. Fred was three years younger than I and a carefree, happy Christian. He had been raised in the church and had a great knowledge of the Bible. I was completely ignorant of the Bible so he was a wonderful help to me. He also went home every weekend and returned with tins of cookies and goodies his Mother had prepared and that he graciously shared with me. I can still taste her raisin cookies. He always called me Louie and does to this day. He's still preaching the Gospel and living in Florida. Another roommate who became a life friend was a Kentucky boy named Charles Delaney. He would later be best man at our wedding and go on to spend his life as a missionary in Zambia,

Africa. Like me, he refuses to retire and continues to preach at the historical Broadway church in Lexington, KY today. Others like John Book, George Melton and Raymond Bennett continue to serve. Lory Bradford of West Virginia retired in Virginia after a long and fruitful ministry and continues to preach.

As we began the study of Acts, the professor gave a true/false quiz to determine what we knew about the book. To the question, "Peter was the first Pope", I put true. After class the professor asked me to stay a few minutes, at which time he lovingly corrected me. Four years later when I walked across the stage at graduation, he shook my hand, smiled and whispered, "Mr. Hall, you learned Peter was never a Pope."

The beginning of my $2^{nd}$ semester in January 1958 brought two loves into my life that I would never get over. The first was that the Scotch-Irish beauty said yes when I asked her for a date. We rode the Bus into the city and had dinner in a nice restaurant called "Georgia's." It was a place where visiting movie stars dined and left their signatures on the walls. I had saved some money for this occasion, but when I looked at the prices on the menu I wasn't sure I could swing it. The food was excellent and I gobbled mine down., but Patsy ate like a rabbit. I wanted to say what I say now, "Are you going to eat that?" But I didn't want to blow it so I said nothing. We then went to the old Albee theater and saw a very romantic movie. We held hands during the movie. It was heaven. Afterwards we had coffee at Walgreens and sat and talked. We rode the bus back to campus, and as we left the bus and walked up the hill, in the darkness, toward the school, we stopped on the path and I kissed her. Oh, what a night!

The second great love was being asked to preach. A small church in Burns City, IN was without a minister and my brother Russell who had moved to a new ministry near there suggested that I might be interested. Russell was forever encouraging me and even got a little support for me from a group called "Kingdom Builders." I hitchhiked the 160 miles, spent the night with Russell and Glenda, and began preaching for the Burns City

Christian church the second Lord's day of February in 1958. No one voted on me or ever even met with me. They were a small group and couldn't pay very much but that didn't matter to me since they weren't getting very much in me. My preaching was pitiful but I was elated. I knew immediately that this was what I had been yearning and thirsting for so long. My brother Russell was most encouraging and helpful in every way. He was excellent in writing sermons and knew the Bible well. He had been in the military four years prior to Bible College and I had been gone for two. It was such a joy to be with him again. I looked up to him in those days and still do. I would have never made it without his valuable assistance.

A good attendance at Burns City was about twenty. This church had been established in 1865. I eagerly hitchhiked back and forth each week to preach for these humble, gentle people. After fifty-three years of preaching, I still think of them. Not one of them is living now, and the building was torn down years ago, but the memory of a young wanna-be preacher, and their patience with him, will forever be vivid in my mind. One of my fond memories was of the oldest member of the church. Her name was Anna Winkelpleck and she was 92 years old. Her husband had been dead for many years and she lived alone in an old house near the church building. One Lord's day in the dead of winter I barely made it to the building because of deep snow drifts. I built a fire in the wood heater and waited, but no one showed up. When I was just about ready to leave the door opened and in crept sister Winkelpleck. I suggested to her that since no one else was coming, we could have the Lord's Supper and go home. To which she replied, "Young man, I didn't walk through that snow to have the Lord's Supper and go home. You've prepared a sermon and I want to hear it. Anyway, you'll never learn to preach if you don't preach." So, on a bitter cold Indiana morning, I preached to my smallest audience ever, a sermon entitled "Hell And Who Is Going There." She sure was determined not to be one of them. She then invited me home for lunch. Afterward, we sat for a long while before the fireplace and she told that young preacher stories too marvelous for words. She had a keen memory of great preachers who had preached at Burns City in its heyday. She told me that during the war the men all left for military service and the women kept the doors of the church open until the war ended. Sister Winkelpleck is buried in the pre-civil war cemetery near by where the church stood.

By the end of my first year at Cincinnati Bible Seminary, Patsy and I were deeply in love. Rather than return to our homes for the Summer we decided to stay on campus. I would go to summer school and continue to work. She would work in a department store in the city. Both the girls and boys dorms remained open year round. She would still have curfew at 9 PM but we would be together all summer. I look back on it as one of the happiest summers I ever had. We were busy but there was time for picnics and visits to parks and attractions in the area. It was a wonderful time for us to really get to know each other. It's no wonder we love the Queen City to this day. Before we registered for our sophomore year I made a trip back home to North Carolina and bought my first car, a 1953 Pontiac. I was almost 24 years of age. The minister at Central Church of Christ asked me to preach on Sunday night. My message was to last 30 minutes. My text was Romans 10:1. When I stood before many friends and family members I was so nervous that I spoke about 10 minutes and was finished. I could hardly tell you my name. It was terrible. It was worse than terrible, it was a nightmare. I was embarrassed and humiliated and vowed never to try it again. I told myself I couldn't speak before a group. Why had I tried? Why could I do this in Indiana but not at home? To add insult to injury, one of the elders offered to give me my old job back at his lumber company saying, "Not everyone is cut out to preach." Before I returned to Ohio I went to visit a godly old saint from the Draper Christian church, brother E.D. (Mickey) McGuire. He gave me a five dollar bill and said, "Louis, if God wants you to preach, He will help you. Go on back to school and do your best." I've always been glad I took his wise advice.

When I returned to college and was showing off this slick

looking Pontiac Silver Streak, Patsy got in it and looking it over, asked me why there were two popcorn boxes in the back seat? It took a minute for me to think, and then I replied, "There's a drive in theater in my hometown and I took a buddy of mine to see a war movie." This has come up a couple of times in the last 53 years but "that's my story and I'm sticking to it."

-

## SKYLINE CINCINNATI CHILI

2 lbs ground beef                              2 (8 oz) cans tomato sauce
1 qt water                                     ½ tsp red pepper
5 whole allspice                               4 T. Chili powder
1 tsp ground cumin seed                        4 cloves garlic, minced
½ ounce unsweetened chocolate (½ sq)     2 T. Vinegar
1 large bay leaf whole                         2 grated onions
5 whole cloves                                 2 tsp worcestershire sauce
1 ½ tsp salt                                   1 tsp cinnamon

In a four quart saucepan, add ground beef to water. Stir until beef separates into a fine texture. Boil slowly for ½ hour. Add all other ingredients. Stir to blend, bringing to a boil. Reduce heat and simmer, uncovered for 3 hours. Cover during last hour if consistency is reached. Chili should be refrigerated overnight so fat can be skimmed from top before reheating. Serve over angel hair pasta (or spaghetti) with grated cheese, oyster crackers, chopped onions and/or cooked chili beans.

This is one of our all time favorite dishes brought to Cincinnati, Ohio by Greek immigrant, Nicholas Lambrinides in 1912. It's named from the view of Cincinnati's skyline which he could see from his first restaurant.

We like it so much we wanted to share the recipe with all who read my book. It will put a spring in your step and make you whistle. Enjoy!

## 1959 - A GREAT YEAR

    We registered for classes and plunged into our second year of study, but halfway through this semester we knew we wanted to be married, so we began planning for that. Our love for each other had grown with leaps and bounds. She accepted the ring I had purchased and we set the date for February 13, 1959. Patsy would go home at the end of the semester and begin getting things ready for our wedding. We would marry at her home church, Hopedale Church of Christ in eastern Ohio. For more than 53 years this church has been a great joy and encouragement in our ministry. Not only is it Patsy's home church but I have long considered it mine as well. I preached there long before I was out of Bible College. No people anywhere have ever offered any more encouragement and showed any greater love to us than this fine church. I have no idea how many times they have asked me to come preach for them. It's always a great joy to go back and meet with them. Great numbers of them have gone to be with our Lord since we first met but their children and grandchildren are there now and we love them as much. There are a number of old timers like me still there.

    We had a small but beautiful wedding, attended by schoolmates and friends at Hopedale church. Being some five hundred miles away none of my own family was able to attend. We had very little money to work with. Patsy borrowed a wedding gown from a good friend, Joye McBride. I borrowed a sport coat and tie from a classmate. A few people had Brownie cameras and took a few snapshots. We have one snapshot of that young, skinny couple and we treasure it. Sometimes when friends are visiting, we ask, "Would you like to see our wedding picture?" Preacher Rusty Morris performed the ceremony. I remember him asking how I planned to treat Patsy after we were married. While I stammered for an answer, he said, "Love her with all your heart and treat her anyway you want to," I didn't see the wisdom in that at first. Patsy's dad, at the last minute, consented to give her away. I suppose I would be putting it mildly if I said that at this time I was not a favorite of Argel McBee's, but in time he would accept me. Patsy was his baby girl and not quite twenty yet. I knew no one would be good enough for her in his eyes. Just wait until the grandchildren start coming. After a short honeymoon trip to North Carolina we returned to Cincinnati and moved into a small apartment where the rent was $15.00 per week. There was no sink in the kitchen, so Patsy had to take the dishes to the bathroom to wash them. (After the children were born I would tell them that I'd fill the tub, toss in some bubble bath and put the dishes in while I took my bath. The girls would scream, but this really didn't happen.) I returned to class and Patsy went to work at the Cincinnati Public Library. I was carrying a full load of classes, and subjects like Hebrew and Ancient History required a great deal of study. The Bible classes continued to be my favorites and I was surprised that my grades in most subjects jumped a full grade now that we were married. I guess that proves what my real major was prior to getting married.

In August before my Junior year I was invited to preach for the Church of Christ at Macon, OH. This rural congregation of around one hundred was some fifty miles southeast of Cincinnati. When they extended the call for us to be their minister, we gladly accepted and moved into their empty parsonage in September. I would commute to school each day and visit and evangelize in this farming community. In order to make my 7 AM class I had to leave home at 5:30 AM. I would return home around 3:00PM. They agreed to pay us $35.00 per week and the house. We would provide everything else. There was no retirement or insurance. One of the men in the church would pay me eighty cents per hour to help on his dairy farm as I had time and opportunity. With a full load at school and a full time ministry I found myself hard pressed to prepare two sermons each week, but somehow I was able to do so. Some of the messages must have been pitiful, but the people were kind and encouraging. We were happy beyond measure. We bought a few pieces of furniture and Patsy made this empty house really look like a home. The furniture was the cheapest we could find and we laugh even today when I tell the story about our coffee table. One night as we sat in the living room I remarked, "Look at that pitiful little coffee table. For two cents I would jump in the middle of it." Patsy got up, found two cents and handed them to me. With that I made one leap and the table splintered into a thousand pieces. The look on her face was indescribable as she picked up the pieces. She never said a word but from then on she believed me when I said, "For two cents..."

There were teenage girls in the church who loved Patsy immediately. She was only 20 when we moved there so when I was away the girls were delighted to come visit with Patsy. They would bake cookies and watch the old black and white TV her dad had given us. We felt very much at home.

I came home one day and Patsy explained that a man from the church had stopped by and given us a package of meat. She asked what it was and he said, "Groundhog." She had accepted it but told me she was sure she wouldn't be able to eat that. I unwrapped it and made cakes and put them on to fry. Soon the kitchen was filled with a great smell. In a few minutes those blue eyes widened and she exclaimed, "That smells like fresh sausage!" I replied, "Well, Charlie told you it was "ground hog." The good people of the church were always bringing things from their garden. The Ralph and Dorothy Beighle family slaughtered a beef each year and always gave us one fourth of it. Ralph was several years older than I and had taken some classes at Cincinnati Bible Seminary. He was such a godly elder and had the Lord's work on his heart constantly. I could not have had a better mentor and tutor than Ralph. He is well in his 90s today and I have thanked him often through the years for the wonderful encouragement he gave me.

Patsy also began getting ready for our first child which was due in late December. When we learned she was expecting I prayed for a son, and on December 19, 1959, just ten months after we were married, Douglas David Hall was born. I named him after one of my heroes, General Douglas MacArthur. We brought him home from the Cincinnati Hospital and put him in a dresser drawer, because there was no room in the inn. No, we put him in a dresser drawer because we didn't have a bassinet or baby bed. For years I would tell him stories about kicking the drawer closed when he would cry. Neither of us could have ever imagined how much joy this son would bring us, and still does. If we thought we loved each other before, Doug's coming only made us love each other more, and now we had someone to share this love with. Throughout his life until he left for N.C. State University where he became an Electrical Engineer, Doug never gave us cause to worry.

My junior and senior years flew by, and on May 10, 1961 I graduated from what is now Cincinnati Christian University. It had been a busy four years but I was amazed at what I had learned and how happy I was preaching. Upon graduation the church raised our salary to $45.00 per week. When I first began preaching I had said I would never ask for a raise and I never have. I'm not positive this was the wisest thing to do. We made it but this was not always fair to the family. I never remember hearing Patsy or the children complain but there were needs (not just wants) in their lives that could have been easily met by the church practicing good stewardship. I greatly appreciate those churches today who take good care of the families they have called to work with them. It has to make their ministry easier. I could tell I had more depth and content in my messages and the delivery came easier. With school finished, I had more time for the church as well as family. I had more time to give to the preparing of messages and visitation in the community.

As I began my third year at Macon, some of my free time might have become an enemy. I had more time to think about things and see them as they really were. I began to experience my first disappointments with things in the church. It dawned on me that as good as they had been to us, the leadership was not really interested in reaching out to the community or beyond. I worked hard at establishing a visitation program but a very few of them were interested. They didn't mind if I went out to evangelize but they refused to become involved. We had no missions program and I hit a brick wall every time I tried to introduce one. It seemed to me that over the years the church had become a small mutual admiration society. We were comfortable and very predictable. We had no vision. They enjoyed being with each other but that was as far as it went. They couldn't understand why I didn't just accept this and be happy. My sermons became more of "whippings" and "guilt trips" rather than encouragement. It was taking a toll on me. For the first time since I had found the joy of preaching, I was starting to dread seeing Sunday come. I had spent four years learning how to grow a congregation and now it wasn't happening. Preacher friends advised me to go elsewhere, but where and how was I to do this? I knew something was wrong, but honestly did not know how to fix it.

In December 1961 I was making a hospital visit in Cincinnati when I drove by the U.S. Army Recruiting Office. Before I knew it I had gone in and talked with the recruiter. Since I would not be officially discharged until October the next year, it would be easy to become active duty again. All I had to do was sign some papers, be examined, and report for duty. With some fear and trembling I signed the papers. I was to report back to the recruiter in sixty days. I had left the Army a corporal. After three months training at Fort Sill, OK I would be commissioned a second lieutenant in my old artillery outfit. My biggest concern was that, unlike during my early military service, I now had a wife and a two year old son. How would this affect them? That night I broke the news to Patsy that I would leave the ministry and go back into the Army. All I remember about her response was that she cried and let me know this was not what she wanted in our lives. Today I am embarrassed and amazed that I could have been so insensitive and thoughtless to her wants and needs. That is not the Louis Hall she knows today. All I can deduce is that it was out of sheer desperation. A week before I was set to resign from the church, a call came from a church in Tennessee, asking if

I would be interested in talking to them about moving there and becoming their minister. Knowing I had committed to return to the military, I still said yes. We drove to Johnson City, TN on that Tuesday and I preached for Buffalo Valley Church of Christ on Wednesday night. Immediately after my message the elders asked if I would come and be their preacher. No voting. No waiting. Will you come? We had fallen in love with this church the minute we walked through the door. Situated in a breathtaking valley with a chain of beautiful mountains in view, it was constructed of rock they had hauled down from the mountain and finished inside with knotty pine wood, bright red carpet, and red padded pews. The members were down to earth, East Tennessee people with that slow southern drawl and the spirit of hospitality dripping from each of them. It was evident that they cared about the lost, and they promised to help me reach out with the good news if I would come. They also had a missions program. They kept that promise throughout our ministry there. The parsonage was nearby, with a huge picture window that provided a view of Buffalo Mountain. It was a ranch style house, finished on the inside with wormy chestnut walls and hard wood floors. We loved it. Before we returned to Ohio the next day, I told them we would move there in sixty days.

How would I be able to do this since I was to leave for Fort Sill, Oklahoma in sixty days? I couldn't believe the mess I had gotten myself into. I was minister of one church, had told another I would come preach for them, and was to return to military service shortly. As soon as we reached home, I made the trip to see the Army recruiter. When I walked into his office he smiled and said, "You're early, preach." Nervously, I explained my dilemma to him. He laughed, took my papers out of his desk drawer and tore them up. He said, "Preacher, I knew you didn't want to leave the ministry so I never sent these papers in. You'll do more good preaching." With that, he shook my hand and wished me the best. It's the only time I've ever wanted to kiss a Southern Baptist deacon. I couldn't believe it. God had brought me out of the biggest mess I had ever made in my life. I rejoiced greatly the entire 50 mile drive back home. Had there been cell phones then I would have called her, but when I walked through the door smiling ear to ear, Patsy knew and greatly rejoiced. She had been praying that things would work out for me to stay in the ministry. She's a great prayer warrior and has prayed for our ministry for fifty three years.

The following Lord's day I announced to the Macon church that we would be moving to Tennessee. As when most ministers resign, it made some glad, some sad, and some mad. It had been a good ministry for us and for them. We had grown in the Lord during this time and now it was time to move on. I wondered if the church attendance would drop off any when we left, but the minister who followed me, Bus Wiseman, had far more ability and talent than I and he took the church to heights I had only dreamed of. He even established a visitation program and got them involved in missions. I have enjoyed going back to Macon to preach revivals and we keep in touch with members to this day.

Patsy McBee, my lovely blue-eyed girl, 1957

Above: Our wedding day, February 13, 1959

Below: Preacher Rusty Morris who performed our wedding ceremony

Above: Revival at Plum Run Church of Christ, 1958. Patsy was the song leader.

Below: With son Doug in Macon, OH, 1961

## EAST TENNESSEE

I was thrilled beyond words to be in Tennessee and to preach for such an excited church. There were many young couples our age and deep friendships were made immediately. One of the teens in the youth group is now my doctor and a good friend at the Veterans Hospital in Durham, NC. People came to be baptized the first two Lord's days we were there and we would rejoice to see more than 40 make decisions that first year. One of the truly great victories was the conversion of an old mountain man named Rassie Jones. He could neither read nor write and had lived a really rough life. While a young man, he was constantly abused and beaten by a drunken father. When he got old enough to fight back he hit his Father with an axe handle during one of their episodes. Thinking he had killed him, he ran and was gone for several years. When he heard his dad was alive he returned to the beautiful hills of East Tennessee and in time married and had a family. He had family members in the Buffalo Valley church and would even attend occasionally, but no one had been able to reach him. We came to love him dearly and it was evident that he loved us. He affectionately referred to Patsy as "Little Patty." When Doug was only three years old, he would say; "Rassie Jones, Rassie Jones, he ate all the meat and left the bones." Rassie loved it. I prayed every day that we could lead him to Christ. I made up my mind that we would love him into the Kingdom of God. I would go to his house, uninvited, and eat cornbread and beans. In spite of our friendship, he would not give his life to Christ, always saying, "I'm afraid I won't be faithful to Him." On Christmas eve of that first year, I had gone to the store for Patsy and as I returned home I passed the street Rassie lived on. At the last minute I turned off and went to his house. He answered my knock and invited me in. I said, "Rassie, I didn't come to eat or visit, but to tell you to bring a change of clothes and meet me at the church house. This is the night I'm going to baptize you." To which he replied, "Alright preacher, I'll be along in a few minutes." And he did, and I immersed him into Christ for the forgiveness of his sins.

He was faithful to Christ and His church until he died. I returned to preach this great man's funeral many years later. That was one of the greatest Christmases I can ever remember, and I think about it every year. The men had constructed a small apartment in the church basement and an elderly lady lived there, known simply as "Aunt Sally." She had no known relatives and the church provided for her. Aunt Sally was blind and so I would often visit and read the Bible to her. She was a quiet and humble lady and appreciated every kindness extended her. When she passed away one morning, some of us went some distance up Buffalo Mountain and dug her grave. I then preached her memorial service and we laid her to rest. I remember my closing remarks to this very day, "Known to very few in life and death, she was certainly known to God, and now awaits that great resurrection when the dead in Christ shall rise and receive their great reward of life eternal."

Events like these endeared me to the ministry and there would be many events in the years to come. The church continued to grow steadily and by the end of the first year, we had to enlarge the building. There were several quartets in the church and others who would do solos and musical specials at every service. It was such a joy to meet with these wonderful people week after week and to have the honor of preaching for them. They were more like family than church members. Bob Watson was one of the most Christ-like elders I had ever met. He knew the Bible and stood for what it said. His wife Kate was such a godly woman and had an upbeat and outgoing personality that just made you feel good being with her. She would often come to our house on Sunday morning, dress the children and take them on to church so Patsy could prepare herself to come. We were quite often invited to their big old farmhouse for her delicious meals. Bob went home to be with the Lord a few years ago and Kate continues to live in the same beautiful farmhouse in Tennessee. Before we left Tennessee I would baptize and perform the wedding of one of their daughters.

On June 12, 1962 God richly blessed us with the birth of our second child, a girl, and we named her Tammy Lou. Like her two and a half year old brother she had blue eyes. It would often be said of Tammy, "She looks like her mother, but acts like her dad." She was a good baby and a sweet child growing up. I often described her as "headstrong, but manageable." She always wanted to know the "whys" of things and did her best to get the last word in any argument. That could often be irritating but in retrospect I believe those traits helped mold her into the mature and successful woman she would become. Even as a young girl, she was always ready to go with her Dad on a preaching trip. We still laugh about the time she traveled with me on a trip into West Virginia. We had driven all afternoon and arrived just at meeting time at the little country church. After I preached, the church took an offering for us and put the cash in a paper sack. On the way home that night I asked Tammy to stay awake, since we had not eaten supper, I told her we would stop for a hamburger and fries. She saw me take the money out of the paper sack and after we had eaten she asked, "Dad, do you think we got enough 'loot' to have some ice cream?"

Tammy brought tremendous joy to our lives and continues to do so today. She's a school teacher with a graduate degree and keeps a busy schedule. Married to minister, Greg Hand, she leads the choir and sings with a quartet at Pleasant Hill Christian in Gasburg, VA. She's the mother of three and grandmother of one with two due in September.

I think of our ministry at Buffalo Valley as truly some of the happiest days of our lives. Our parents were living then and we got to visit them several times each year. We were young and our health was excellent and we were busy and happy in the lord's work. East Tennessee was in the middle of the Bible belt and it was easy to witness and lead people to Christ. I would study in the mornings and head out to visit after lunch each day. Sometimes I would leave the car at home and just go door to door, walking and inviting people to Christ. That was not thought strange in those days, and I can only remember a house or two where I was not welcomed. What thrilled me was the number of people that I was baptizing into Christ. It was not unusual to have these people being visited to come forward in a church service weeping over their sins, confessing Christ and obeying Him in baptism. Forgive me for being negative but I don't remember the last time I saw anyone weep over their sins.

Once on a door-to-door visitation I came to a large house with a white picket fence. My knock at the door was answered by an elderly man in his eighties. I learned he was a retired Engineer on the Clinchfield Railroad. As we talked he told me he was not a Christian, and living about a mile from our church he often wondered why no one had ever come to tell him about Jesus. On this hot, July afternoon he listened to every word I told him about Jesus and on that following Sunday, I baptized him into Christ. He was faithful until he went home to be with the Lord a few years later. I preached his funeral message.

From our bedroom window I could see the tops of houses high up the side of rugged Buffalo Mountain. I wondered about the people who lived up there and if anyone had invited them to Christ. The next day I made my way up the mountain and stopped at the first house I saw. Seeing no signs of life, I knocked and called out, "Anybody home?" A small boy of perhaps ten years old answered the door and I asked, "Is your mom or dad home, son?" He replied, "Yes, they are in the kitchen. Come on in." As I stepped into the kitchen, I don't know who was the most startled, me or them, for there on the kitchen table was perhaps 10 gallons of moonshine whiskey. They were busy pouring it into pint Mason jars when I interrupted them. Without hesitation I introduced myself as the preacher and invited them to church. They asked the time of services and said they knew some of our members and would try to attend. As I made my way back down the mountain, I wondered if any of the members they knew might be customers. Maybe I'd need to prepare a new sermon. As far as I know, they were not raided while I lived there. That was probably good for me. A few months after this incident, I was rabbit hunting with one of our deacons and he told this joke while we were hunting:

"The Revenuers went up on Buffalo looking for a still, and

seeing a small boy standing in the road they said, "Sonny, tell us where the still is and we'll give you a quarter." To which he replied, "give it cheer." They said, "We'll give it to you when we come back." The young boy grinned and said, "Mister, if you go up to that thar still, you ain't gonna come back." I always wondered if that could have been a warning to me. Anyway, I ain't talking, except in this book and I know you won't tell.

In the early Spring of 63 Patsy informed me that God would bless us with our third child in the fall, and on September 10 Brenda Gail was born. We named her after a sweet girl in the church. The third time was not only charm, but I finally had a brown-eyed child. We all welcomed her with great joy and felt our family was really complete. We now had three children under the age of four. As I look back, it had to be exhausting for Patsy to take care of three young children and stand by my side in this growing ministry, but I honestly never remember hearing her complain. She was always a wonderful mother and gentle and loving to the children. The three of them greatly adore their mother.

Brenda's tender and caring spirit was evident early in her life and continues to this day. Even as a child she was full of sympathy for the sick and discouraged and tried to lift them up. She was especially caring toward the elderly. She could always make us laugh and often did at her own expense by sharing some supposedly dumb thing she had done or said. It's no wonder that she would become an emergency room nurse at a large hospital and be held in high regard by coworkers and patients. She is almost nightly with those who are suffering and dying and feels their pain and that of a grieving family. She has a great ministry in nursing. Like her brother and sister, Brenda has filled our lives with joy. Her brilliant mind sometimes amazes me. Her love and caring overwhelm me. She and husband Thomas Haynes gave us three loving grandchildren. I refer to her as my "brown eyed girl," and I do love her dearly.

## REVIVALS AND GREAT MEN OF GOD

It was about this time in my life and ministry that I began getting calls to conduct revival and evangelistic meetings in other churches. I loved it and knew immediately that this was where my heart was in ministry. Carter county had 27 churches of Christ and in just a few years I had preached meetings in all but three of them. It was also during this time that I had the great privilege of knowing and working with some great men of faith who are no longer with us. Henry T. Reynolds was a great evangelist and church planter. I worked with him in many revivals and in planting three new churches in Johnson City, TN and Lenoir and Morganton, NC. When he left Tennessee to preach in Louisiana I went there on several occasions to preach for him. He had a tremendous singing voice and would often lead singing when I preached. His singing of "The Holy City" always gave me goose bumps. Traveling to a preaching point one winter afternoon our car broke down on top of a mountain between North Carolina and Tennessee. While I worked under the hood trying to get the car fixed Brother Henry sang all the verses of that great hymn with all the voice and volume he had. I had never heard before nor since such an anthem to God as it echoed off the mountains. My eyes tear up just remembering him and what a blessing he was in my life. I saw him for the last time about a year before he died. He came to hear me preach revival in Tennessee. When he greeted me he hugged me and said, "Aw, Lou. You went and got old."

John B. Hall was an evangelist with East Tennessee Evangelizing Association. He was a "firebrand" and had preached all over America. He preached without notes and carried a small pocket size New Testament. His preaching style was like that of an auctioneer and it was known to be straight down the line. Brother John was witty and always quick with an answer. Once he and I were having breakfast in a restaurant in Elizabethon, TN when a preacher from the non-instrument church of Christ came in. Seeing brother John, he approached us and began to rant concerning the use of the piano in worship. "How dare you tell people there will be musical instruments in heaven?", he exclaimed. John waited until he finished and then, smiling, he said, "Pard, I think you have the wrong John. That was John, the Apostle in the book of Revelation." Johnny, as he was known, was a great soul winner and led many thousands to Christ during his more than 45 year ministry. Many of the methods I have used in personal evangelism during my ministry I learned from this great man of God.

O.L. Mankymer was another great traveling evangelist during that time. He was a huge man with a booming voice and no patience for foolishness in the Lord's work. He was quite controversial and a stickler for the truth. Like brother John B Hall, his sermons would often last an hour or more. These men insisted that no one get up and walk around or that no child talk or cry out. It was not at all uncommon for them to call disturbers down from the pulpit. During a week of revival, he requested only one meal per day and he wanted that at noon. He had an enormous appetite and could put away an entire chicken or five pork chops at one sitting. It was amazing the food he consumed at this one meal. He ate nothing else throughout the day but after preaching and before he went to bed, he always ate a pint of Ice Cream. Brother "Mack," as he was known, taught me many things about preaching and soul winning, and I was blessed to have known him and rubbed shoulders with this great servant of God.

One night brother "Mack" finished the last service of revival in a church in a tobacco farming area in East Tennessee. He and I were standing talking when the treasurer of the church interrupted us to say to brother Mankymer, "Preacher you preached a lot this week against smoking and tobacco. I just thought you might want to know that this check I'm giving you came from the sale of tobacco." Suddenly Mack's face turned blood red. He took the check, tore it in little pieces and handed it back to the treasurer. He then got his hat and walked out the door. These old firebrand preachers were like the prophets. They could not be intimidated and were not for sale. People repented of sin in those days and wept over them. Do you think we're missing something in this 21$^{st}$ century?

Melvin Sparks was another preacher of the Gospel who had a tremendous influence on my life and ministry. When I first met him in 1964 he was preaching at a small church in Hamlet, NC. I had gone there to conduct revival. He was a great personal evangelist and a prayer warrior second to no one I have ever known. He was a large man with a booming singing voice. On a number of occasions he would sing in revivals I was conducting. If you went to his house to visit him his wife Marge would often say, "Preacher is praying. You're welcome to wait but it could be several days before he's finished." She wouldn't interrupt him. He might pray for an hour or he might pray all day.

I must give credit to this great brother in Christ for first introducing me to foreign mission work. He begged me to go to Grand Bahama Island and preach the Gospel. He believed the world was lost and the Lord's command to go and preach was to us. My life would never again be the same after I went.

In the spring of 1965 I went to Elwood City, PA to conduct revival services and met a man that would become a great joy to me and my family. J. Fenton Messenger of Canton, OH was to be the song evangelist that week. He was a large man about six feet and two inches tall and weighed around two hundred and fifty pounds. He had a smile larger than himself and his "arf, arf" laughter could be heard a block away. Just being in his presence lifted your spirit. He had served as Chaplain during World War 2 and could share many stories about that experience. He had graduated from Phillips University in Oklahoma. Fenton led singing with a xylophone. He played the French Horn and many other instruments. Before I would preach each night, he would bring out a box he had labeled, "God's Mystery Box", and from it he would perform some trick with a powerful lesson for life. The children loved him. After this first meeting I would call him to lead singing for my revivals in many places across America. All these men and many others helped me greatly in my efforts to be a preacher of the Gospel.

While I preached at Buffalo Valley, I began getting calls

from other churches to be their preacher. In those days, it was not uncommon for a visiting pulpit committee to show up, unannounced, to listen to me preach. This always caused alarm for those who really loved me and may have offered some hope for those who loved me less. I was happy where I was and had little interest in going anywhere else. But in May of 1963 I was asked to preach a week on Grand Bahama Island. This was my first time to preach outside of the U.S. and it would do something to me that would shape the rest of my life. Patsy wanted to make this trip with me and I greatly wanted her to go. After all, we had belonged to the Missionaries of Tomorrow group in college but her Doctor advised against it since Brenda was due in another four months, so I went alone. It was wonderful to finally preach in another country, and I had the feeling this was the beginning of something I would be doing a lot. Since English was their language it was easy to preach there, and several obeyed the Gospel, being baptized in the beautiful Atlantic Ocean. This was my first fruit in a foreign country and I knew I wanted more. God knew I needed growth and maturity and so it would be eight years before I'd leave the U.S. with the Gospel again.

It was during this time that I made one of the greatest mistakes I had ever made. I decided to leave the located ministry in Tennessee and travel in general evangelism. I spent little time praying about it and therein was the tragedy of it. I told God what I wanted to do and expected him to rubber stamp it. Had I sought God's will in this matter, I would have stayed on in this fine church until such time that God was ready for me to launch out. There was weeping in this mountain church when I resigned. Two children had been born here and the church had wrapped their arms about us the entire time we lived among them. I had not been gone a month until I knew I had run ahead of God and that I would pay a price for this. We put our furniture in storage until we decided exactly where we would live, and Patsy and the children traveled with me in revivals. It was exciting to begin with but soon the road began to take a toll on us all. I had never put a price on preaching and haven't to this day, but sometimes we barely made expenses. Doug, who wasn't even five yet, broke my heart one night after saying his prayers, when he said, "Daddy, I want to go to my Tennessee home." I wept bitter tears and remember thinking, "Louis, you've turned your family into a family of Gypsies." I once again apologized profusely to Patsy and promised God that I would never again rush into anything without first seeking His will. I have tried hard to keep that promise. Never again would they be without a permanent home, no matter how I had to sacrifice.

I was a young and unknown preacher so when the revival season ended just before winter, I found myself without work. We moved to Hickory, NC where I worked with Henry Reynolds in establishing churches at Lenoir, Morganton, and Hickory. We held services in our rented house in Hickory and I went to work for Pinkerton Detective Agency as a guard at a local hospital. I worked the midnight shift which freed me to evangelize during the day. We did this for several months while we sought out God's will for our future. I stayed exhausted from lack of sleep. When a call came from First Church of Christ in Coldwater, MI, we made the long trip up and I met with the leaders and preached on the Lord's Day. I can't say we were really excited about the move there, but it was a place to preach and settle our family in a more permanent place, so we accepted their offer and moved there. I had preached revivals there and knew it was a place where we could win souls, and we did. That church provided an excellent salary so soon we had caught up from being with inadequate income for months. Doug would be going into kindergarten in the fall and was quite anxious to begin. He had always had a thirst for learning and was reading at second grade level already. Coldwater was a good church, but had its share of internal problems, and it seemed that we were always having to put out little fires that had been smoldering for years. I resumed my evangelistic calling immediately after arriving there and as is always the case, people began responding to the Gospel. Someone introduced me to an older couple, the Shrimers, who were staunch Roman Catholics. I asked if I could come and study the Bible with them in their home and they were delighted, explaining that they had been in the church since they were infants, but had never studied the Bible. In fact, they didn't even own a Bible. I took them each a Bible and we studied for four weeks, one night each week. On the fourth week they both confessed Christ as Savior and I took them to the building and immersed them both into Christ. They were faithful as long as I was acquainted with them. That first year we were steadily seeing new people obey the Gospel and the church grew in number. Many dear friendships were made that have endured through the years. By the end of the first year attendance had increased to around 200.

Coldwater was a pleasant place to live during spring, summer, and fall, but the winters were brutally cold. Snow would begin falling in November, and you seldom saw the ground again until spring. In January of 1965 there was a period of about three weeks where the temperature never got above freezing, and several of those days were below zero. It was necessary to use an electric dip stick to drop in the engine block to prevent the oil from getting so thick that the engine would not start. On several occasions we had to delay funerals of members because of the bitter cold and frozen ground. Doug started to school that fall and loved it from day one. One morning when the car wouldn't start he cried and asked us to call a taxi so he wouldn't miss. He sure didn't get that from his Dad.

I stayed busy with the ministry at Coldwater and invitations to preach revivals continued to come in. I conducted meetings at Battle Creek, Lansing, and Allen Park, and being on the Indiana line I conducted meetings in Indianapolis and Angola. I had earlier established myself as an evangelist in Tennessee, North Carolina, Ohio, and Pennsylvania, so churches in these areas also invited me back to preach. I found my heart lighter and my happiness greater when I was on the road in meetings. I missed Patsy and the children when I was out, but knew immediately that my preaching was better and my joy in the lord far more evident. Coldwater was financially stable and paid a really good salary, so I knew they would have no problem getting another preacher. I wanted to preach where no one else wanted to go. This time we both discussed it and prayed about it for six months. We would be absolutely sure it was God's will before we made another move. After we began praying about God's will for our lives we were contacted by a very small and struggling group of believers in High Point, NC. They had a small building on the north side of this furniture city, a city at that time of 78,000 people. They asked if we would come and meet with them and see if it might be possible to work with them in building up the Body of Christ in this place. They also stated they were willing to wait as long as necessary if we thought we might be interested. We sincerely sought God's will in this. It bothered me that we had been at Coldwater only about two years. This was not even long enough to get to know the people and there was really no reason to leave. They seemed to love us, even though their hospitality was somewhat different from that we experienced in Tennessee, and there was plenty that needed to be done here. I called High Point and told them We wouldn't come. Delbert Davis, one of the elders, asked me to give it some more thought and prayer and to call him if I changed my mind. He again told me they were willing to wait. More than a month passed and I was unable to get the challenge of a struggling, new work in a city of 78,000 out of my mind.

Louis and Patsy in
Coldwater, MI, 1965

## HEADING SOUTH AGAIN

After thinking about it and asking God's guidance, we called Northside and told them we would drive down and talk with them. We spent the night with my parents in Draper and drove over to High Point, which was about an hour away. The meeting with the small group of believers at Northside was good, and Patsy and the children were in agreement that this would be a good move. They explained that one reason they had been unable to get a preacher to come is that they could only afford to pay $50 per week and provide a very small 850 sq. foot house. No insurance, retirement, car allowance, or any other benefits. That meant I would be taking an $80 per week cut in salary, plus all the benefits I was receiving. They did say they would allow me to work at a secular job to supplement my income and to preach as many revivals as I desired, and when the church grew and they were able, they would raise my salary to a living wage. We accepted their offer! The part about the revivals probably made the difference. As we closed out our ministry in Michigan and moved back South, there was no doubt in our mind that this move was the leading of the Lord. We still believe that today.

I knew it would be a struggle to live on so little, but believed with all my heart that God would provide for us and use us to do a good work for Him in this place. This sure proved to be the case. After we moved into the small house, I remember telling Patsy and the kids that the house was so small that we would have to go outside to change our mind. Brenda asked, "Really Daddy?"

On the very first Sunday, nine people stepped forward to identify and place membership with the church. The excitement and joy was unreal and we knew the best days for this church were ahead. This little band of believers would grow to more than one-hundred and fifty in just a few years and we would indeed enjoy some of our happiest days in this church.

On Monday morning after our first Lord's day, I drove into town looking for a job. Just on the edge of the city I came to a stop light, and as I waited for the light to change I saw a man watering the grass at a funeral home. I called out good morning to him and asked him if he needed any help. He smiled and asked, "What can you do?" I answered, "I can do it all except embalm, and I can help you do that." As the light changed he called out, "Pull in and let's talk." It turns out this man was Harold C. Davis, owner and operator of Davis Funeral Services. He was looking for someone to drive the ambulance and assist him in conducting funerals as well as cut grass, wash cars, and whatever else came along. If I was interested, he would pay me $75 per week for four days, Monday thru Thursday. I would have Friday thru Sunday off and every night. This was ideal for visitation in the evenings when most people were home. I would have Friday and Saturday to study and prepare two sermons for Sunday and a lesson for Wednesday night. I shook his hand and went out to finish watering his grass. I now had my salary within five dollars of what we had left Michigan making. Harold Davis was a great guy to work for. Being a devout Quaker he had some deep convictions and a sincere faith in God. I enjoyed my work since it put me in contact with the public and gave me the opportunity to witness to many people. I had no experience or training as an ambulance driver. This was before the days of Rescue Squads when funeral homes sometimes took care of this. The attendant who rode with me knew the city so when a call came in, away we would go. We never lost a patient and I rather enjoyed the experience of driving an emergency vehicle. One really funny experience I had was when I was supposed to deliver the body of a deceased man to a little church in the country, some thirty miles away. He was to lie in state from 2 to 4 PM before the memorial service. I left the funeral home in plenty of time to make it to the church house, but got lost on the way and drove around and around looking for it. Seeing he was going to be late for his funeral, I finally flashed my lights at a State Trooper and with a police escort, we arrived at the building only ten minutes late. That night I told the kids, "The guy was late for his own funeral, but never said a word."

  We truly loved it in High Point. We lived in a neighborhood where there were plenty of kids and there were quite a few kids the age of ours in the church, so the children made many new friends. After a year the church purchased a nice brick ranch style house several miles out in the country, and we all were elated to be there. In a short time I had baptized the next door neighbors, and another lady just down the street placed membership with the church. The church was growing fast and was full of love and sweet fellowship. Northside was blessed with people who knew the Bible and there was no shortage of people willing to teach. During most of our years there we had a visitation program that took place one night a week. A goodly number of men and women took part in this and many new people were reached with this program.

One of the sweetest women in the church was Eschol Campbell. Our family was often dinner guests in her and her husband's home. Mrs Campbell was diagnosed with cancer and spent months in the Hospital. It was during these long months while Patsy and I took turns sitting with her at night that Patsy decided to study Nursing. One night Eschol slipped quietly out of the room and went home to be with her Lord. I preached her memorial service and Patsy enrolled in the Nursing program at Guilford Community College. She was older than most of the students just coming out of high school but ranked near the top of the class the entire time of her training. We still didn't know it, but God was slowly grooming us for foreign work. How valuable her nursing skills would be once we got on the mission field.

The six years at Northside were happy and productive for us all. Patsy would graduate near the top of her class in Nursing and the children would be well launched in school. They were happy and growing and God was blessing us all with good health. Many souls were obeying the Gospel at Northside and many more in revivals I was conducting throughout the U.S. The church had come from about thirty to some one-hundred and fifty and was able to pay a full time salary. I quit my job at the funeral home after about a year and worked full time with the church.

One of the things that contributed to the rapid and steady growth of the church was a pattern I had set at the very beginning of my ministry. I would rise early each morning and go to the church office to study and prepare messages and would spend the afternoon in visitation. At least one night per week I would be in someone's home to teach. This was always by appointment. Since Sunday and Wednesday nights were church nights, this left me four nights each week for family. As I look back on it more than 35 years later I realize it was one of the wisest things I did. We were always together for the evening meal and it was a valuable time for family togetherness. Though our children are adults now they have remained faithful Christians and led all eight of our grandchildren to become Christians.

Each Monday I would arrive at the church office at 7 AM and conduct a live phone devotional and prayer time. We had no recording equipment. From seven until around eight thirty I would answer the phone by reading a short passage of scripture, making some brief comments, and praying for the caller. I received a good response from this and believe it was something that helped the people in their walk with Christ. The little "grandma" and oldest member of the church was Mae Davis. She called every Monday morning and did her best to engage me in conversation. I refused to be distracted and always hung up after the prayer. She was not a little irritated that the preacher hung up on her every week and she told me so every Sunday.

It was a practice of all the Christian churches in the area to conduct a Missions Rally in the Spring each year. Some eight to ten missionaries would be invited to the area and they would rotate among the churches each night showing slides and telling of their work. It was truly the highlight of the year for me. As happy and busy as I was at the time, I dearly longed to be going to some of these far away places to preach. Aged veteran missionary Edgar Nichols was working in Ghana, Africa and made me cry as I saw his pictures. I could have never known that Patsy and I would set foot in Ghana almost 40 years later. Art and Ruth Morris shared their thrilling work in South India. He made such a plea for workers that both Patsy and I were touched and we talked about it until the wee hours of the morning. The next night we went to where he was speaking and told him we would be willing to become missionaries to India and help him in that far away place. Immediately he began to explain that if we came out to India it would be necessary to put the children in a boarding school nine months of the year and this school was located 600 miles from where we would live. We would only have the kids three months of the year. Our "call" to India ended then and there! Whatever we would do for the Lord, we would do as a family. I have since met missionaries who lost their children to Satan and the world while living in one place and the children in another. I concluded years later that Art was not really looking for more workers for South India since he had hundreds of Nationals trained to do the work but it sure made a great Missions message to make such a plea. I would hear this plea from many foreign workers in the years to come. Maybe it was meant to convey the message; "If you aren't willing to come, you will surely send money." Little did I know that my thoughts about working in India were not over and I would make a number of preaching and teaching trips to that country over the years. Even as I write there is an invitation on my desk to return there during 2012.

Our family in
High Point, NC
in 1967

Family portrait from 1970 in High Point, NC

## GOING HOME

It was mid way into 1971 and I was happy and busy and entertaining no thoughts of leaving Northside for another ministry when a late night phone call changed all that. One of the elders at Draper Christian in Eden, NC was calling to see if I might be interested in moving there to work with the church. I promised I would talk to Patsy and the children and get their feelings and after we prayed about it I would call him back. We laughed later when I told someone that after hanging up the phone I told Patsy to start packing while I went and prayed about it. After discussing it we all agreed that this could be a good move. I wanted to return to my home church for a lot of reasons. I knew most of the people and loved them. This is where I had accepted Christ more than twenty years before. I had never felt like I was finished with Draper Christian when it split and my family left. I truly wanted to make a contribution and was sure that I could. Mom and dad were still living and I could stand on the church steps and see their house less than 200 yards away. I had grown up in this town and knew many people whom I believed could be reached with the Gospel, and many were. All but three of my eleven brothers and sisters lived here and I had enjoyed little fellowship with them in the past twenty years. The brick house I had been chased from when it was under construction had long been the parsonage and that's where we would be living. About a week later I called brother Dennis Steagall and asked when I could come for a trial sermon. He said there was no need for that and that the church would vote the following Sunday. I received 126 yes votes and 1 no. Years later one of my dearest friends and strongest supporters confided that she had been the one who voted no. When I asked why she had voted against me, she explained it was because of what Jesus said in Matt.13:57; "Only in his hometown and in his own house is a prophet without honor."

I resigned my ministry at Northside the next Sunday. Things were different there than when I came. The church was much larger in attendance and had sufficient offerings to call another preacher and pay him well. They had a nice three bedroom, two bath parsonage and elders and deacons in place to lead. Our dear son, Douglas had become a Christian. In a rather short time they had called Elbert and Jackie Lilley to that ministry.

We said farewell to our friends in High Point and moved to Draper the last week of June 1971. The kids went to Ohio and spent a few days with Patsy's parents on the farm while we arranged for the move. They would be at their new home in Draper the week of the 4$^{th}$ of July. It was the only move we have ever made where the movers wrapped and packed everything. We ate our breakfast that morning and left the house as it was. They moved it to Draper and put it in the rooms we had designated it for. Well, almost anyway.

We had no way of knowing that the next years at Draper would be the most effective located ministry we would ever have and one of the happiest. A great number of people would give their lives to Christ. Tammy and Brenda would become Christians here and all three would graduate from the same school I had graduated from. Each of them would meet and marry their life's mate in this town. Neither could I have imagined that this would be my last located ministry and would launch me into thirty-seven years of general evangelism and foreign mission work. I continued the practice of study and sermon preparation in the mornings and visitation in the afternoon and evenings. It was a pleasure beyond description to stop at Mom and Dad's while out visiting and enjoy a cup of coffee and some rich fellowship.

It would be impossible for me to record all the wonderful ways God blessed our ministry at Draper. The church grew in number and there was excitement and joy as more and more people became obedient to the Gospel. Bill Underwood, his wife Peggy, and their three teen age sons were all baptized at the same time one Lord's day morning. Bill had lost his sight in a hunting accident years before, but his spiritual sight was restored that day. He serves as an elder at Draper Christian today. Bill Jarrett and Julian Slaydon were men I had known as a boy and now I had the great joy of immersing them into Christ. In later years I would conduct funeral services for both of these faithful men. I had grown up with James Jones, and after teaching him one afternoon he also obeyed the Gospel. Elwood Fayne was a good moral man but had never obeyed the Gospel. One morning he called to say he was ready and obeyed the Gospel and united his family in Christ. He would go on to become the treasurer of the church. There were many more who came during this period. I believed then that a church could not help but grow when the preacher set the pace in personal evangelism. I still believe that today.

One really funny thing happened to me shortly after I arrived there, though it was quite embarrassing at the time. One of my old friends from the days before I became a Christian showed up at church one Sunday. As I stood in the foyer with two elders greeting the worshipers as they arrived Teddy came through the door. It was obvious he had been drinking. He said, "I had heard you made a preacher so I wanted to come see if it was really true." What he said next made me catch my breath and made my knees buckle. He grinned a silly grin and said, "Remember that time we got kind of wild and you drove my Model "A" Ford into a tree?" The two elders just grinned and walked away. They never mentioned the incident and neither did I until now. One of the wonderful things about the good people in Draper church is that they never regarded me as "the poor boy who grew up in sight of the church but never attended." They accepted me as one who had been washed in the blood of Christ and was now a new creation in Him. They are still that way.

Our son Doug and I have always been close and engaged in quite a bit of horseplay when he was growing up. Patsy was continually saying, "Somebody's going to get hurt!" Or, "You're going to break something." One Saturday I had just had my shower and was drying off in my bedroom, wearing only my underwear. Doug came into the room, picked up a wet towel, and began stinging me with it. I warned him to stop but he continued so I ran after him as he went through the door. Seconds later we bounded into the living room where two older ladies of the church sat talking to Patsy. They were shocked and Patsy was mortified. I quickly retreated back to my bedroom where I found Doug down on the floor roaring with laughter. I waited until the ladies left and went out to face Patsy. All she could say was, "I've told you boys and told you boys. How many times have I told you boys?"

A strong youth group developed during this time with sometimes more than 50 meeting on Monday night. Barbara Sanders organized and led a group of younger children in a program she called "Bumble Bees". It made a lasting impression on these children and contributed greatly to the good of the church. Barbara and I had attended elementary and high school together. She and her husband Joe were faithful members, and we vacationed with them for several years. After a lengthy illness a few years ago Joe went home to be with the Lord. I had the honor of going home and speaking at his memorial.

When we first went to serve at Draper the church was giving 10% of their income to missions. In those days that was considered "mission minded." After a year I encouraged them to raise it to 20%. It was wonderful. We were supporting four foreign missions and three at home. I gave weekly reports of our missions, informing the members what their mission money was accomplishing on the field, and I preached on missions once each month. We made sure that missionary newsletters were on hand and the members kept informed. I don't see this much anywhere these days unless it's about camp or one of our bible Colleges. For the most part our people cannot name our missionaries or the fields on which they labor. That's too bad. When did you last hear a young boy or girl say they wanted to be a missionary when they grew up?

In early 1972 Ken and Eunice Salyers called me saying they had committed to go to Vietnam and were having trouble raising support. They could go immediately if they had the support. They asked if there was a chance we could help them. I asked for a meeting of the elders and we discussed what this would mean to the church. The Salyers needed an additional $400 per month to be able to go. Calvin Willard, a sweet spirited and kindly elder spoke. He said, "If we are sending men there to fight, we ought to send men there to preach the Gospel." This would mean raising our mission giving to 40% of the offerings. When the men voted, it was a 100% favorable vote. Ken and Eunice left within a month. They were the only missionaries we had in Vietnam at that time, and they stayed until the cease fire came a year later and all missionaries were forced to leave.

At one time we had six young men and one girl enrolled in three of our bible colleges. It was such an exciting time when they would come home for a few days and share with the church the things they were learning and doing. I continued to conduct many revivals and was unable to accept all the invitations that came in for meetings. God was giving great victory in these meetings and I continually had the feeling that this is what God had set me apart to do. But I had tried this in 1965 and fell on my face. Why would it be any different now? Besides, I had promised Patsy that I would never again put her and the children in this situation, so I put it out of my mind.

In the summer of 1972 LaVerne Morse spoke at Draper and stayed in our home. His entire family had spent many years in China, Tibet, and Burma until they were ordered out. They were working now in Thailand trying to reach back into the countries where the doors were closed. LaVerne was now teaching missions at Cincinnati Bible Seminary and was also heading up Southeast Asia Mission. During his short stay with us he asked me to make a trip into some of those countries to preach, teach, and evangelize and work with the nationals on the fields. I would be gone for six weeks and would work in India, Burma, and Thailand. Since Vietnam was between Thailand and Hong Kong and since we had recently sent the Salyers family there I could also spend two weeks with them. I jumped at the chance and asked the elders if I could be gone for this long period. Since we were supporting Ken and Eunice it made it easier for them to approve my going. All I remember is someone asking me, "You do know there is a war going on in Vietnam, don't you?" Today that would no doubt alarm me but at age 37 I don't remember giving it a thought. When word got out that I was making this trip many friends wanted to help, and Draper Christian supplied what was lacking.

I left in early November on Pan Am's around-the-world flight on a giant 747, flying to New Delhi and taking the long train ride to mid India and the city of Damoh. For two weeks I preached and taught Bible classes. The only drawback was that I did not speak Hindi. Vijai interpreted for me. He and his beautiful wife Pushpa were gracious hosts and I enjoyed staying in their home. Each night she would place a mosquito net over my bed. It was cool in the early morning so we would breakfast outside in the sun. By lunchtime the sun would be scorching hot. This was before bottled water was so readily available, and being forewarned not to drink the water in India, I was always thirsty. We made evangelistic trips by Jeep to Bilaspur and Jabalpur where I preached and taught classes during the day. I visited a leper colony and after speaking was invited to have lunch with these pitiful people. Rice with bits of meat was served to each of us on a large leaf. We ate with our fingers. It was a simple meal. As I looked at these lepers with eyes, ears, and fingers missing and some without hands or feet, I thought, "Thanksgiving is not far off in America and most Americans will be dining on turkey with all the trimmings and today we are eating rice and who-knows-what." On our way back to Damoh late that night everyone had fallen asleep but young Ajai, his Uncle Stanley, and myself. As the Jeep rounded a curve our lights shone on a beautiful Bengal tiger. The driver stopped and we watched it for a few moments before it was gone. I had never before nor since seen such a beautiful animal in the wild. The last message I delivered at Damoh that year was on the love of God. A lady about 60 years of age came forward and we gathered at the river for her baptism. After she was immersed I asked her through Dr. Lall why she had become a Christian after being Hindu all her life. She replied if God loved her enough to give His son, she wanted to serve Him. Before leaving Damoh I was able to make a trip to Agra to see the beautiful Taj Mahal. As I looked at this magnificent structure I remembered how my school teacher, Mrs. Edwards, had first told me about it and showed me a picture in a book.

I said goodbye to the Christians at Damoh and boarded a train for the all night ride east to Calcutta. I would be here two days before my flight on Pan Am to Rangoon, Burma (now Myanmar.) I was not prepared for my arrival in Calcutta. I did not know one person in this city of millions. I might have known a half dozen words in the Hindi language. Death, sickness, and poverty were everywhere I looked. Hoards of beggars pounced on me at every turn. Great numbers of entire families were living under culverts and in large cardboard containers. Someone told me that many are born, live, and die on the streets of Calcutta, never having a roof over their heads during their lifetime. Though I could not accept Catholicism, I did have a greater appreciation for the work Mother Theresa was doing in that nightmare of a city. I found a cheap hotel, and upon checking in the clerk handed me a pitcher of water. It was cool and looked clean and clear so I downed it in just a few swallows. I had been drinking Cokes to be on the safe side, and this water was the first thirst quencher I'd had in days. I asked for a refill on the water, went to my room, barricaded my door, and fell exhausted into bed. Sometime through the night I awoke with my stomach on fire. Between vomiting and diarrhea I never slept anymore that night. I was sick all day the next day and unable to take any food. Patsy had packed medicine for me and by bedtime the diarrhea had subsided. I was able to eat a few peanut butter snacks and drink warm Coke and rested well that night. You would think that would have taught me a lesson concerning the water but I would make that mistake again and again in the years to come.

I was still weak on Thursday morning but checked out of the hotel and caught a taxi to the Calcutta International Airport. Pan Am 1 was on time and I departed for Rangoon, Burma as scheduled. I had tears in my eyes as we lifted off and I saw the squalor of that city and the masses of lost people. How would we ever do what our Lord told us to do at the pace we were going? About an hour into the flight the stewardess brought food trays.

By then I had eaten enough rice to last a lifetime, but to my surprise we were served sliced turkey, potatoes, and green beans with a nice dinner roll and dessert. It was the first meal I'd seen like this since leaving home. Prior to the meal everyone was given a steaming hot towel and it was as delightful as the wonderful meal. While I was enjoying the meal, the stewardess, without my asking, set a sparkling, cold glass of champagne on my tray. I do not drink alcoholic beverages today nor did I then but I reasoned that if a little wine would help Timothy with his stomach problem maybe a cold glass of champagne would help mine. I don't recall that it did or didn't.

I was met at the Rangoon Airport by brother George Than Win who was Burmese, and brother Edward Shawn Bill who was of the Chin tribe in northern Burma. Security was tight and it took me a while to clear customs. It seemed the officials wanted to know everything about me. Why was I here and what were my plans while in Burma? My visa only permitted a 7 day stay in Burma and I dared not tell them I was here to do missionary work. All foreign missionaries had been ordered out of this socialist country in 1965. One of the brothers from the North told me that at the 1971 Christmas gathering of churches of Christ/Christian churches in the north they had reported a membership of 40,000. When the Morse family left in 1965 they had reported 15,000 members. That would mean without the presence of a missionary they had added 25,000 souls. I would challenge the people of Haiti and Grenada with this many years later. In all our mission work since that time I have stressed the importance of nationals reaching their own people. The work in Grenada, West Indies is completely self supporting, self propagating, and self governing because Jim Newman and I taught them this from the beginning.

My short week in Burma was spent teaching leaders from the North who had come down to Rangoon for this seminar. I was allowed to go no farther North than Mandalay, but classes were held in Rangoon every morning and afternoon. It was a joy to fellowship with these brothers in Christ and I felt humbled to be teaching them. These men had all paid a price to be followers of

Christ and they could have taught me much about serving Him. We shared a meal of rice and beans every day and rejoiced to be together.

One day during that week the city was suddenly filled to capacity with people from all over Burma. I learned that for that day only a part of the toe bone of Buddha was on display in the Shwedagon Pagoda. Standing 325 feet high, this gold leaf covered pagoda dominates the skyline of the city. It boasts also having a piece of the robe and eight strands of hair from Gautama, the historical Buddha. I was amazed that thousands of people stood in the boiling sun to see these. Burma was 89% Buddhist with less than 4% claiming to be Christian. That would include anyone who believed in God.

With a lump in my throat I said goodbye to our dear brothers in Burma and flew to Bangkok, Thailand. There I was met by Peter Sutjiban and David Kalin, two Lisu tribesmen now living in Chiang Mai in northern Thailand. Both of these men were from Burma and had fled there because of persecution. They would later come to America and study at Cincinnati Bible Seminary. We spent the night in a Missionary Alliance guest house and took an early morning train to Chiang Mai. For the next ten days I preached and taught classes to a small group of Christians. About mid-week I was shocked when two of the men from the seminar in Burma showed up. They had walked from Burma into Thailand through the "back door," as they put it, to continue to study. I learned it was a common practice for entire families to travel back and forth between the two countries through the "back door." This turned out to be a great way to get Bibles and other supplies into northern Burma.

One of the Lisu preachers asked me to go with him to a Lisu Christian village in the mountains. It was about a day's journey by car, boat, and a long walk through jungle and rough country. Upon arriving we were warmly welcomed, and I spent two days teaching and visiting with these humble followers of our Lord. I remember it was like stepping back hundreds of years in time. They had no electricity or modern conveniences of any type, no phones or radio. They lived in houses of thatch, sitting on posts. I had never seen a people with so little and yet so happy. As we sat around a campfire one night the moon shone bright above us and I mentioned the marvel of Neil Armstrong's visit to this heavenly body. This had taken place almost three years before and they had not heard it. I smile as I recall that they didn't really seem impressed by the news.

Before I would reach home again Patsy would get a letter from one of the preachers expressing his thanks for my coming and saying, "Brother Hall suffered much in the jungle." We still laugh at that.

I arrived in Saigon, Vietnam on December 4. Two hours after my arrival the city was hit with a Viet cong mortar attack and all who could went to a bomb shelter. I had arranged previously to stay at a Christian Missionary Alliance guest house until I could travel the 180 miles north to Dalat where Ken and Eunice Salyers were in language school and working with a small group of believers. That night I recall standing on a balcony and watching the sky light up in the distance with flashes from rockets or mortar rounds. I then recalled one of the men at Draper saying, "You do know there's a war going on there, don't you?" Dalat is in the central highlands of Vietnam and a seven hour bus ride from Saigon. I was told there was often fighting between Saigon and Dalat and that the bus was often delayed. Even though it cost more I opted to book a seat on Vietnam Airlines which would take about an hour. Ken and Eunice met me at the airport. It was good to see them and they were happy to see another American. I learned they were quite homesick and were experiencing a good bit of culture shock. Dalat was a beautiful city with pine trees and red soil. It was the flower and vegetable capital of the country and had been a playground for the wealthy French in earlier years. I conducted nightly Bible studies with this small group and spoke for them on the Lord's day. One very moving experience was standing outside at night and hearing the B-52's high above as they flew north to Hanoi on their nightly bombing raids. I cheered that the Yanks were taking it to them. The Air Force flew 741 B-

52's raids over Hanoi during "Operation Linebacker" in December. Fifteen of these great planes were shot down and many crew members died. Those that survived were captured and placed in the infamous "Hanoi Hilton." Jane Fonda and I were in Vietnam at the same time but not for the same purpose. The citizens of South Vietnam believed this would soon end the war because of the damage done in Hanoi by the bombing. Railroads, bridges and valuable infrastructure had been destroyed. But when a bomb hit a hospital only a mile from the airport and killed a number of doctors and nurses a cry went up from the liberal press. Even NATO screamed about it. Such an outcry went out that President Nixon called a halt to the bombing. Many military leaders believe we were on the brink of victory when the bombing ceased. Who knows but what Vietnam might have been a free country where the Gospel could be preached?

My greatest contribution in Vietnam was to encourage these young missionaries who were so far from home and in a country that was at war and without Christ. As I left I promised to return the following year, but that wasn't to be. Due to the turn of events in the war Americans began leaving the next year. Ken and Eunice returned to America in 1973 where he continued preaching and has just retired from the ministry after leaving Vietnam 38 years ago. He told me in a phone conversation recently that he had received only one letter after returning home and they had written, "We are hungry, really hungry." It has long been my dream to return to Vietnam and that beautiful mountain area of Dalat. I would dearly love to announce the Gospel once more in that land where the people suffered so much and our precious young men and women in uniform paid such a price.

Home was a welcome sight as I flew into Greensboro on December 15. Patsy and the children were there to meet me and I cried as I held them in my arms again. What I had seen and experienced would take a toll on me emotionally in the days to come. I was physically exhausted and drained emotionally and would wrestle with depression for several weeks, but I knew that my life would never be the same. After this first trip to Southeast

Asia I continued my ministry with Draper Christian and did my best to put the mission field out of my mind but this was easier said than done. This trip had deeply affected my life for missions.

    For the next two years I continued to preach and serve at Draper Christian. Souls continued to obey the Gospel and the church grew to around 200 in attendance. Still, I had this gnawing feeling that I wasn't doing all God wanted me to do. I had seen the field first hand. I had witnessed the dead and dying on the streets of Calcutta and the masses throughout Southeast Asia who had never been invited to Christ. I had watched the sky light up from mortar rounds at night in Vietnam and walked within feet of dead South Vietnamese who had been cut down by the Viet Cong, and the Christian church had only one missionary there. I wanted so much to give full time to this type of work, but I couldn't shake the memory of failing in 1965 when I tried to launch out the first time.
    In the summer of 1973 I went to Hamersville, OH to conduct a week of revival for Tom Friskney who had been one of my professors at Cincinnati Bible Seminary. Hamersville is only thirty miles east of Cincinnati, and during the week LaVerne Morse called and asked if I would drive in and have lunch with him. He wanted to talk to me about a great need with Southeast Asia Evangelizing Mission. During lunch he asked me if I would be willing to join the team and represent SEAM. This would involve speaking in churches concerning the work in Southeast Asia and making trips there to preach, teach, and encourage. I could arrange my own schedule and they would provide leads if needed. I agreed that we would pray about it and promised to get back with him in a month or so. Patsy and I did pray about it, and in October when I went to Atlanta, GA to preach revival services I had the opportunity to spend some time with Jim Vernon. He had recently left a fine ministry in the Winston Salem area to work with the street people of Atlanta. He called his ministry Jesus Place Inner City Mission. It was a ministry to hurting and homeless people on the streets of Atlanta and continues to do a

good job today. Jim graduated to eternal life with Jesus a few years ago. Big Jim was the dearest of preacher friends. He was from the same hometown as I and we had worked in several revivals together. There was no other preacher that I had more confidence in than Jim. When I told him about my invitation, he asked, "What are you waiting for? You'll have the best of two worlds. You can travel in revival meetings in America and do mission work abroad."

As soon as I arrived back home Patsy and I sat down to count the cost. I wouldn't make the same mistakes I had made ten years ago. I had just turned 39 years of age. I had ten more years experience and had conducted revival meetings in 12 states. Upon contacting some of these churches they agreed they could use me for meetings in the coming year and several agreed to support us financially. Patsy's home church, Hopedale Church of Christ in eastern Ohio, was the first to send a gift of $50. They have not failed to send a monthly gift for our mission work in the 37 years since then. With less than $400 in savings we applied for a loan to buy a house and were approved immediately. This was a nearly new three bedroom, two bath brick ranch on the west side of town. It had a large lot with fruit trees, carport and paved drive. We smile today when we remember the price.... $21,500.

One night in mid October Patsy and I retired for the night and lay in bed talking, praying, and still trying to decide if I should resign at Draper Christian and go full time with general evangelism and missions. Suddenly we began to see daylight and realized we had talked all night about this. I got out of bed, dressed, had my morning coffee and walked over to the church house where I sat down at my desk and typed out my resignation. Immediately I felt as though a thousand pound weight had been lifted from me. I did not regret it an hour later or a month later or 37 years later, not ever, and not even a little. I believe to this very day that it was one of the best decisions I ever made and that God was directing it all the way. I believe the time was right and that's why it didn't work out nine years before. Had I known where God would lead me and that thousands of souls would obey the Gospel in America and countries abroad I'm sure I would have had another sleepless night. After typing out my resignation and signing it, I prayed, "Dear Father, I don't know where this is all heading and I'm scared to death, but you promised to be with me to the end of the age. I'm claiming that promise this morning. Amen." Not even one time since the morning I prayed that prayer has God ever failed us in any way. We never missed a meal or failed to make a house or car payment. We've never become wealthy in worldly goods, but we have never lacked. "Our God has supplied all our need's according to His riches in Christ Jesus." We have watched literally thousands of people come to Christ and have gained a host of friends far too numerous to count. We are rich indeed.

On the first Sunday in November 1973 I announced to the church that we would be leaving. To many it was no great surprise and though happy for me, the vast majority of the church was saddened by the news. Truth be known, it may have made a few glad. That's nearly always the case. But to the surprise of many it made some folks mad, and several families left the church for another church in town. In later years most have returned to Draper Christian. I see them on occasion and our conversation is always one of friendliness and congeniality. I've always been glad for that. Whenever I'm asked about my home church and our ministry there, I always answer by saying, "It's a fine church and I am happy that I served there."

Above: Family photo in Draper, 1971

Below: Louis with bible college students from Draper Christian Church in Eden, NC, 1972

## "INTO ALL THE WORLD"

We moved into our new home toward the end of November. Patsy and the children were elated. They didn't have to change schools and never missed a day in the move. We had been married fifteen years and this was our first home. Patsy enjoyed being able to paint and paper and decorate as she wished. I closed in the carport and made a nice den. In the spring we would plant a lot of flowers. In fairness to the minister that followed me at Draper, brother Harold Morris, we considered moving our membership elsewhere but Harold insisted it would not be a problem so we stayed there and continued the sweet fellowship we had enjoyed. A couple of years later Harold left and Draper called a "pharaoh that did not know Joseph" to be their next minister. He was not comfortable at all with a former minister attending, though due to my travels I was not there that much. He was never unkind but his discomfort was evident. So in consideration to him and his ministry we moved our membership to Leaksville Christian. My younger brother, Joe, had graduated from Bluefield College of Evangelism and began a ministry at Leaksville in January 1977. Joe is a talented preacher, both in word and musical ability, so it was great being with him and his wife, Marlene. The building was only a couple of miles from our home. I had conducted several revival meetings here and knew most of the people. It was here a few years later that both Doug and Tammy would be married.

I don't have the words in my vocabulary to describe how it felt to finally be doing what I knew God had set me apart to do. Unlike my earlier attempt at this in 1965 my schedule for 1974 was chocked full. When word got out that I was available invitations for revivals, Faith Promise meetings, and Men's Retreats came at a pretty steady rate. I went first in early January to Joliet, IL and conducted a Missions Rally with First Christian church. From there I came home and preached close by in the area for the rest of January. When not scheduled to speak anywhere on a particular Sunday I would often be asked to supply for someone.

Every week was different and my free time was really free time. Dad had suffered a stroke a few years earlier and could no longer drive. Since he was pretty much confined to home it meant much to him for me to come by after a meeting and share it with him. He would always ask, "Did you preach that sermon on the second coming?" He cried easily and would sometimes do so when I told him of people obeying the Gospel. I would often take him for a drive down by Cascade Creek or the Dan River area. On one such ride he told me I was the best preacher of his three preacher boys. I laughed heartily since I knew he had told both Russell and Joe the same thing.

By the summer of that year I had conducted revivals in North Carolina, Virginia, West Virginia, Georgia and Ohio. Most churches back then had annual revival meetings and some had two each year. Seldom was there a meeting that someone failed to come to Christ, and to see eight or ten come was not uncommon at all. During these meetings I would also be given the opportunity to present the work of South East Asia Mission. There was only one thing I disliked about this new venture and that was being gone from Patsy and the children. More than once I would leave on a Saturday morning for a week of revival hundreds of miles away and cry for the first 15 or 20 minutes of the trip. Had we had cellphones, computers, or a GPS in those days they would have made a great difference. I took comfort in the fact that the children were happy and doing well in school. They would never move again until they were out of school and on their own. During this time they developed deep friendships that have endured to this day. Doug works in the office of a company in Raleigh, NC where one of his childhood friends, Miles Gillie works. Doug would marry Tammy's best friend, Bonnie Hall. Tammy would marry the boy across the street and Doug's best friend, Greg Hand. Brenda would marry a friend of Tammy's and classmate Thomas Haynes. Complicated? It was to us also, but it was wonderful. They have given us eight grandchildren and one great grandson (so far) and raised all of them to know the Lord. They are a joy to Patsy and me.

In September I received an invitation to speak in Tulsa, OK. I was to speak at a Men's Retreat for the Tulsa area churches on Friday night and conduct a Faith Promise Missions Rally for Osage Hills Christian church on the next Sunday. My assigned topic on Friday night was, "How to get the job done." I don't know if that large group of men learned anything new from me that night on how to get the job done, but I always suspected that what they really wanted to know was pretty much what we want to know today, that is, "How to get someone else to do the job." God has made it clear as to how we can get the job done. The commission actually says, "As you are going into all the world, preach the Gospel to all creation." Most all of us are going somewhere every day... to work, to the store, the bank or post office. We can still get the job done if we take the name of Jesus with us. Unfortunately, the church of the 21$^{st}$ century is about "Super Pastors." They have studied in Super pastors college and know more than anyone else how to get the job done. If after a few years with us they fail to get the job done, we can always get rid of them and find someone else to do it. For some reason it seldom dawns on us that God wants us all involved in getting the job done.

On Sunday I preached a message at Osage Hills entitled, "White unto Harvest." Their goal for missions was $30,000 and when all the pledges had been received they totaled $34,000. The bulk of this would be used to support Mid-India Mission at Damoh, India. Dr. Vijai Lall was director of this work. I had visited him in India in 1972 so I knew something about what he was doing and the great need there. This work is well known today and has impacted thousands of lives. It is under the leadership of Vijai's son Ajai who was 13 years old at that time.

September and October were prime months for revival so I was kept busy at these. In late October I began making preparation for my second trip into India and Southeast Asia. As we began 1975 I looked back on our first year in general evangelism and mission work and rejoiced at what God had done. I had conducted 17 weeks of revival meetings, spoke for several

Faith-Promise Rallies, conducted two Men's Retreats, worked in two weeks of Christian service camp, and spoke in three of our Bible colleges. I had raised funds for SEAM and helped in the planning stages for a Bible college to be launched in Chiang Mai, Thailand. Best of all I had witnessed a good number of people give their lives to Christ.

I have long believed our ministry has been unique in that we divided it between evangelism at home and abroad. There really is no difference between the two. I have never felt it was necessary to neglect the work abroad while we did the work at home. Neither do I think it wise to neglect the work at home while we work abroad. We can and should be doing them simultaneously. Our mission work and all its projects have been and are now supported by contacts we made in the nearly one thousand revivals I have conducted in thirty four states. Between the work in Haiti and Grenada we have had more than 250 Americans visit us to teach, preach, practice medicine, hold dental clinics, conduct VBS, and build buildings. Many of you reading this visited us on the field and saw what we were doing and wanted to help. God bless you.

Stew Worthley of Indiana visited and saw us without transportation so he went home and raised $12,000 to buy us a new truck. Ed Hewitt visited and gave us $5,000 to finish a project in Haiti. He and wife Linda continue to help to this day. Jonathan and Becky Parker of Gretna, VA visited and set up a free dental clinic. Del and Anita Crabtree of Kentucky have made numerous contributions and even visited us on the field. I could go on and on with names of those we first met in revivals who became "Rope Holders." Then there are many who have never seen and still believe. My nieces, Hope Mullins and Kimberly Nance, along with Kim's daughter, Beth made 172 dresses to send to Africa with us. How happy this made the young girls at the orphanage. William and Beth Sawyer bought all the windows for our building in Grenada after it was destroyed by hurricane Ivan. May God bless you all richly. He has your names even if they don't appear here.

# EVANGELISM IN AMERICA

I regret that I didn't keep records of all the meetings I conducted and much of what I now write is from memory but these are a few I do have written records of. Some of you may well remember some of these and if you became Christians then, I would rejoice to know it.

## Oct.31-Nov.5, 1976 - Salem Church of Christ- Salem, VA

I was anxious to conduct this revival because the minister was Roy B. Miller. He had been the minister at Draper before I ever attended church or became a Christian. Roy was sold on the importance of visitation and was the first to make a real effort at reaching my parents, Clyde and Dorothy Hall. After several visits with them he baptized them both. Had he not reached them I might never have become a Christian since Dad led me to Christ. This revival was especially tender for me since Dad had just passed away on July 10. I put my hand on Roy's shoulder and said "Brother Roy, I believe Clyde Hall is in Heaven tonight and I will forever love and appreciate you for telling him about Christ." We both cried. Mom has since gone home and Roy is in a rest home in Salem.

We had a tremendous week of revival with seventeen making decisions for Christ. Ten made the good confession and were baptized. Seven others came to place membership or for rededication. One night I walked to the pulpit and there lay a slip of paper that said, "Brother Hall, will you please go visit this man?" His name and address were on the paper. After church I showed the paper to Roy and he said he didn't know who he was or who had asked us to visit him, but that we would go see him the next day. After lunch we found his home and knocked on the door. Neither of us knew him or what we would find at this house. The door opened and a man around sixty years of age stood there with an open Bible in his hand. Roy introduced us and said that someone had asked us to visit him. He explained that we were in revival at Salem church of Christ. The man looked shocked and for few seconds he was silent.

Then he said, "Well, I don't know who asked you to visit me and I don't even know where the church of Christ is, but you could not have come at a better time." He went on to explain that his wife had died a few months back. He had never been involved in church but her death had got him thinking about God. While we were knocking at his door he was trying to read the Bible and find out what he needed to do to be saved. The rest was so easy. Brother Roy opened his Bible and taught him about Christ. We both answered his questions as best we could. That night Roy baptized him into Christ for the forgiveness of sins and gift of the Holy Spirit. Do you ever wonder just how many people in your community are trying to figure it all out and just waiting for someone to come and teach them? Oh! what great opportunities we have in this great land of America to share Christ with others.

> When in the better land
> before the bar we stand,
> how deeply grieved our souls will be.
> If any lost one there
> should cry in deep despair,
> "You never mentioned Him to me.
> You met me day by day.
> You knew I was astray,
> Yet.. You never mentioned Him to me."

## September 6-11, 2001 Acre Chapel church- Plymouth, NC

Patsy and I were excited as we drove to eastern North Carolina for this meeting. It has long been a favorite place to preach. I had been there on many occasions. The meeting began on Sunday night and the first two nights were well attended. Quite a few friends from area congregations had been there and there was excitement in the air. It was such a joy to see our close friends, Jay and Pammy Bell. They had been and continue to be such encouragers and supporters of our work. Pammy sang on the night of the tenth and did her usual great job. We were staying at the Earl Baynor cottage on the creek and after breakfast the next morning we turned the TV on to catch the news. We watched in horror as planes were flying into the twin towers in NYC. We stayed glued to the TV for most of the morning. And though they were not anywhere near New York we felt a need to call all the children, and we did so.

I spent several hours in the afternoon writing a new sermon to preach that night. I knew the mood would be different from the first two nights and I wanted to share something uplifting and encouraging. Sure enough, the people were somber as they gathered to worship. They were quieter and the singing was not as spirited. When I stood to preach I gave no introduction or shared no funny stories as I often do to loosen up the audience, but read from 2 Chronicles 7:14. "If my people, who are called by my name, will humble themselves and pray and seek my face and turn from their wicked ways, then will I hear from heaven and forgive their sins and heal their land."

I don't know how many were encouraged by this message but I was, and as long as I live, when someone asks me where I was and what I was doing on 9/11/2001, I'll remember.

## October 2-7, 1964 -Elizabethton, TN

I think I set some kind of record during this revival. Located a short drive from Elizabethton, TN Pogie Christian church was like going back 50 years in time. A country church in the Tennessee hills, they had a pot-bellied stove to heat the building, an outhouse, and a well with rope and bucket for drawing water. It was reported that when evangelist John B. Hall held a meeting here he had been critical of one of the old men of the church for bringing his coon dog into the building. To which the gentleman replied, "Come on Blue. If you ain't welcome, I ain't welcome and anyways, I'd a sooner hear you bark as to hear him preach."

The statistics for that week of revival were that I preached 7 times, had 7 baptisms, ate 5 chickens, and had 3 flat tires. This was the meeting where another old gentleman told me he had been thinking about being ordained as a minister. When I asked what had brought him to that decision, he replied, "Well, I ain't got nothing to do but sit on the porch all day. I can run up and down like you do. I might as well be a preacher." I'm still trying to figure that one out.

Savannah, GA , April 10-17, 1970

I was cutting the grass on Saturday when the mail man stopped and I paused to look at the mail. I read in the South Gardens church paper that Louis Hall was to begin a revival there the next morning. Somehow I had either forgotten about it or failed to write it down. I screamed for Patsy to pack my things and in about an hour I was on my way to Savannah. The late Ben James was the preacher there. He was the dearest of friends and a great man of prayer. We baptized two on the Lord's day and on Monday morning we set out for a day of visitation. It was the normal thing in those days that the visiting evangelist and located minister would spend the day visiting before services each night. There are a few exceptions but seldom do I see that happen today. I'm told it no longer works. Funny how it worked back then!

Ben had a long list of people for us to visit, and at the top was a lady named Mary Bishop. She was 35 years old, divorced, and lived with her mother on the other side of Savannah. We drove to her house, knocked on the door, and her mother answered explaining that Mary guessed we might come by so she left. She had no idea where she was and when she would return. When we got back in the car to leave Ben put his hand on my shoulder and said, "Brother, let's pray." Those of you reading this who knew Ben would remember that he talked to God just like he talked to us. He told the Lord that we really wanted to talk with Mary about her soul and that she was somewhere in Savannah and we didn't have time to run all over the city looking for her. He went on to say if God would guide us to her we would do our best to reach her. As we drove off I remember thinking this would be like finding a needle in a haystack. Fifteen minutes later I asked Ben to stop at a drug store and let me get some cough drops for my ever-hoarse throat. When we walked in the door he said, "There she is." Mary was sitting in an empty booth at the soda fountain. We were able to talk with her and encourage her to do what she had been thinking about. That night Ben baptized her. When I asked him later if that amazed him he answered, "Well, if the Lord could bring Phillip and the eunuch together, I guess he could bring us and Mary together." What a great lesson on how God answers prayer.

September 27-Oct.1, 2010 -Christian Hope church, Pinetown, NC
We were in the midst of a great revival in spite of flooding all over East Carolina. Many roads were closed. I was staying in a motel in Washington, NC and several nights the water would almost flood out my truck as I drove back and forth. Several had responded to the Gospel but there was one man we were especially praying for. His dear wife was a Christian and member at Christian Hope, but he had never obeyed the Gospel. This man had attended every night and was under conviction but would not step out. Before the end of the meeting I preached a sermon entitled "Barriers on the road to hell." I pointed out that God had made it hard for us to be lost by placing barriers between us and that terrible place. One of them was the Bible. We sang the invitation song and he failed to respond. It was then that the minister, Reggie Braziel did one of the most daring things I had ever seen a preacher do. He spoke to the church saying he was not afraid of losing his job for this but that he was going to make it hard for anyone to leave tonight without Christ. He then walked to the door in back, laid his open Bible down and walked back to the pulpit. Then with great emotion he said, "If you leave here tonight without Christ, you'll have to step over the word of God to do so." You could have heard a pin drop. A few of the people looked shocked or maybe embarrassed. We had the benediction and Reggie and I walked to the back where his open Bible lay. The people began to make their way out of the building and I watched the man in question. His face was red and he appeared to be angry. When he approached us he stopped short of the Bible

and said, "Preacher, if you think I'm going to step over this Bible tonight, you're wrong. I'm ready to become a Christian. Come back in and baptize me." And so we did. Oh! What a great night of rejoicing this was. May God give us a holy boldness as we try to snatch souls from the fires of hell.

June 14-19, 1987 -Patrick Springs, VA Stella Christian church.
My diary for this weeks of revival reads, "A great week of revival with a really super group of Christians. On Sunday we had 3 come to rededicate their lives to Christ. Monday-2 baptisms-Tuesday -2 baptisms-Wednesday -2 baptisms-Thursday -1 baptism -Friday - 2 baptisms. A total of 13 decisions. What a singing church. The Stella Girls, a quartet made up of a mom and three beautiful daughters sang several nights and did an outstanding job. Enjoyed preaching here so much."

May 26, 1966 -Allen Park MI
"Dear brother Louis,
please accept this small gift out of great appreciation for having had you in our presence for the revival. I am more than proud to have brought both Catholics and non-Catholics to hear your powerful preaching from the Word of God. I want you to know that you have really impressed their minds.
May God bless and keep you in His care.
Sincerely,
Laura King"

April 7-12, 1963 - Elizabethton, TN -
Borderview Christian church.
In an old scrapbook I found this announcement written by Richard Piper, minister at Borderview church in 1963: "It is certain you will not want to miss a single night hearing this dynamic young evangelist, Louis Hall. Louis is 26 years of age, married, with two children. He is well known in East Tennessee as a man that will get the job done. During his short ministry at Buffalo Valley the church has added 38 new members and built a

new wing and baptistry on the building. You'll be surprised at this young man's down to earth and dynamic preaching." We had 9 souls saved during this revival.

September 19-25, 1966- Shattalon church of Christ-
Winston Salem, NC

The following appeared in the church paper, "The Winner" on Sept. 19, 1966: "We were happy that the revival with Louis Hall got off to a good start. A wonderful crowd was in attendance and we rejoiced when Mrs. Janet Watson came forward to confess Christ and be baptized. Her husband, Don also came to rededicate his life to Christ. Brother Hall is a powerful preacher of the Word and began his series of messages with a sermon on the "Rich Fool." There's still time for you to attend this great meeting. Come on out." I remember this as a wonderful week. Six others came to accept Christ.

September 21-October 2, 1964 -Church of Christ-
West Union, OH

This two week revival holds a lot of memories for me. My brother Russell was minister of Georgetown, Ohio Christian church so I would get to visit with him during the meeting. The late Bus Wiseman was minister at West Union and was one of the most effective visitation ministers I have ever known. I knew upon going there that we would contact a lot of people during these two weeks and we did. A total of seventeen souls made decisions. Eleven by confession of faith and baptism. Six others came to place membership with this young church. As I write these memoirs I'm continually reminded that in the meetings where large numbers obeyed the Gospel, we were always involved in one on one teaching and personal evangelism. Today I constantly hear preacher brothers say that the revival just doesn't work anymore. Is it possible that they don't work because we quit working in them? Years ago when preacher Jack Ballard, minister of the East Point church in Atlanta, was asked the secret to a growing church, he replied, "Three things spell success for a growing church, See the people, see the people, see the people."

Another sweet memory I have of the West Union meeting is that Patsy and our three children were present with me and we were housed for these two weeks in the Adams County Children's Home. It was a home for homeless or neglected children. Many of them were waiting to be adopted or taken as foster children. Our children loved playing with the other kids and felt right at home with them. Those old enough to be in school went to the public school in town. The younger ones had this big house to play in throughout the day. We ate our meals in a huge dining hall. Brenda was one year old and the older kids carried her around like a rag doll. Tammy bossed the other kids just like she did her sister. (Love you Tammy) When the meeting ended Doug wanted to stay at the orphanage. It would be my best chance of getting rid of the boy but I'm so glad I didn't.

## May 3-16, 1964- Elk Mills Christian Church, Butler, TN

My good friend Buford Cole never went to bible college to become a minister. He just loved the Lord, knew his Bible, and wanted to serve. When this little country church located in Carter county Tennessee needed a preacher and was much too small to pay a livable salary, Buford volunteered to preach for them. It was sheer joy to be with this dedicated brother. Tall and raw boned, he had a smile as big as Texas and had never met a stranger. He had fought with the second infantry at Normandy and been awarded a purple heart and bronze star. His sweet wife Ruth was just like him, tall, outgoing, and always smiling. They were a perfect fit for Elk Mills Christian. During our two week revival we rejoiced to see 15 obey the Lord. After service each night we would gather on the banks of the nearby Elk river where someone would set a bale of straw on fire to give light and the converts would be immersed in these cool waters. As I record these events tears fill my eyes when I remember the saints singing on the banks of the river, "Jesus paid it all. All to Him I owe. Sin had left a crimson stain. He washed it white as snow. I am coming Lord, coming now to thee. Wash me, cleanse me in the blood that flowed on Calvary." I don't know when I last heard that song. It had a message and plea that we are hurting for today.

It seems to me those were simple times and these were just plain, down to earth folks who loved the Lord and struggled along on their way to Heaven. Church was not so much about numbers, programs and organization but more about Jesus and how He could save the sinner. The emphasis was not on doing everything inside the church building but on how we were to live out in the world. Buford and Ruth Cole had a tremendous influence on my life and ministry. They long ago went to be with Jesus. I'm looking forward to our reunion in Heaven. It's so easy for me to see in my mind's eye that Tennessee preacher coming to greet me with that great smile as he throws his long arms around me and with that Tennessee drawl says, "Welcome home Lou." I miss him. It will be Heaven.

## Aug. 3-9, 1977- Double Creek church-Dobson, NC

Two humorous things happened during this one week revival. I arrived on Saturday and was taken to an old couple's country home where I was to stay that week. They went to bed at 8:45 each night and since there was only a curtain separating my bedroom from theirs and the curtain hung down a foot from the floor, I had to turn my light off when they did and go to bed. It was still daylight. I have always been a late night person and even now I go to bed around 1 AM. (I'm writing this at 1:30 AM.) You can imagine how I tossed and turned for hours until sleep finally crept up on me. To complicate things they got up at 5 AM sharp. She would prepare a full breakfast of eggs, country ham, gravy, and (on several mornings) grits along with biscuits. I am a one bowl of corn flakes man with gallons of strong, hot coffee. They were not coffee drinkers. I don't know if they even had a coffee pot. By 6 AM breakfast was finished, the dishes washed and put away, and we were sitting on the front porch of this little white frame farm house watching people whiz by in their cars on their way to work in Mt Airy or Winston Salem. "Oh! will Friday night never come?"

We were happy to see two come to be baptized on Tuesday night and the crowds, which had been slim, were picking up. I preached on Wednesday night, "Be sure your sins will find you out." As I stood at the door after the service, a man walked out, shook my hand and said, "That was the most pitiful preaching I have ever heard." Taken back by that I said, "Oh?" He went on to tell me what a poor job I had done and that I should get a job doing something else. I then asked him if he preached and he told me he didn't preach but he knew good preaching and mine was not good. I then quoted an old mountain preacher friend, "I like the way I can't preach better than the way you don't preach." I learned a few months later his wife had left him because he was seeing another woman. I guess his sins had found him out.

<u>November 3-8, 1963 -Central church of Christ-Mt.Vernon, OH</u>
It was an exciting time for me as I drove from Tennessee to Ohio for this revival. My good friend and classmate from Cincinnati Bible Seminary, Richard McBride was the minister. Dick was an avid coon hunter, good preacher, and an outstanding personal worker. I knew we would have a good meeting and we did. On the Lord's day we saw two baptized and one place membership. On Monday as we went out for visitation Dick did something I had never before or since see anyone do. He took the church's membership roll with him. We visited the many people on the roll who no longer attended. As we went into the homes he would simply ask them what their intentions were and if they wanted to remain members. As I recall it made a few people angry and they told Dick to remove their names. But to others it was a shock to learn they had quit. One man declared he had not quit and Dick replied, "Well, you haven't been there in months. You don't give any support to the church or take part in any of the activities. What else would you have to do to quit?" It was deathly quiet for a few moments and then he said, "Well, I guess I have quit, haven't I?" He then promised to get back and he did.

This was an outstanding week of revival, and a few all-night coon hunts after church several nights didn't hurt it any either.

## May 22-27, 1968-Preaching for the Pope in Allen Park, MI

Not very many evangelists and none that I know have ever preached revival for the Pope, but I had that pleasure. Wade Pope, another former classmate from Cincinnati Bible Seminary was minister at Allen Park in Michigan when I went there to preach. Several families united with the church during the week. I stayed in the home of Bill and Carolyn Cabel who have remained lifelong friends.

During the week I preached a message about Hell and after church someone told me there was a small town of about 200 in the southern peninsula of Michigan called Hell. The next day we drove down. The sign on the edge of town read, "Welcome to Hell." It was a small tourist town and several people were milling around the gift shops when I went to the car and got my Bible. I walked up to the intersection and began to read and preach. In about five minutes the town cop came by and said I would have to have a permit to preach on the street. When I asked where I could get that he said that office was closed for the day.

When I returned to North Carolina I remember attending a meeting of the area preachers. During announcements I told them I had just had a revival with the Pope and we both went to Hell where I tried to preach.

## Oct.5-19, 1970 -Elwood City Christian church- Elwood City, PA

Another quite memorable two weeks of preaching took place in the northeast town of Elwood City, PA in 1970. Clarence (Rusty) Morris was minister and my good friend J. Fenton Messenger of Canton, OH was song evangelist. One night he sang that beautiful song, "Beyond The Sunset" and dedicated it to a man in the audience named Virgil Brock. I was not aware that Virgil had written this song and more than 500 more. He sold "Beyond The Sunset" to the Rodheaver Music Co. for only $25.00 He was 83 at the time and would live to be 90. He is buried in Oakwood cemetery in Warsaw, IN. Take a moment to

Google "Virgil Prentiss Brock" and you'll see the most unusual tombstone you've ever seen. We had eleven people baptized those two weeks. A week later I received the following letter from the elders at Elwood City.

Oct. 28, 1970
Dear Lou,
We would like to express our thanks and appreciation for your efforts on our behalf during our recent revival meeting. We are mindful of the sacrifice relative to your family and work for having come to us. We feel you did an excellent job and that the Lord will reward each and every effort in His own way and time. Thank you again for everything. May the Lord bless and keep you as you labor in his service.

Yours in Christ,
Elders at Elwood City

Robert W Walker
Charles F Jenkins
Herb Blankley
Harry O'Brien

As I write this I am aware that all of these good men, Rusty, Fenton, Virgil, Robert, Charles, Herb, and Harry are all gone from this life. I'm truly excited to know I will meet them again Beyond The Sunset where there are no sunsets.

March 2-16, 1977 El Paso, TX
I had first met John Paul Biliter in a revival at Martin, Kentucky. He was a retired railroad man and had been minister at the Martin church. A year after I met him he moved to El Paso, TX hoping the change in climate would relieve him of pain from severe arthritis. He wrote and asked me to come for a revival so I made the long 1500 mile trip to this Marty Robbins town.
For two full weeks I kept an unbelievable schedule. I taught a

class on Personal Evangelism at El Paso Christian College from 9 to 11 each morning. From 12 till 2 I worked with brother Ed Wekerly across the border in Juarez, Mexico and at 7:00PM I preached revival at the Christian church in El Paso.

God blessed the two weeks with souls saved both in Texas and Mexico. I failed to keep a record of how many. After about a week of being in El Paso, homesickness set in and I had never missed Patsy and the kids so much. I remember to this day that at night the March wind would howl around the corners of the little house where I was staying. That sound seemed to add to my homesickness. After 34 years I still remember those nights and don't believe wind has affected me like that before or since.

I also remember a story John Paul told me about an old gentleman he worked with on the railroad. John described him as a grouchy and disagreeable sort of fellow. One day as they were getting off the train at the end of their run, the grouch said, "I'm going home and if the old woman don't have dinner hot and on the table, I'm gonna jump all over her and if she does, I ain't eating a bite."

October 2-8, 1990 Philippi church of Christ Creswell, NC

This fine congregation is located in far eastern North Carolina. This was the first of several revivals I preached there, and brother David Sikes was minister. His mother in law had died and his father in law, Dean Floyd Clark, had moved to Creswell and attended Philippi church. He was a retired professor of Greek from Johnson Bible College and quite a scholar and preacher. At times he came across to me as quite comical without meaning to be. After I would preach each night he would invite me over to his house saying, "I'll pop us some corn and we'll look at some scripture." I supposed he was just lonely and wanted some fellowship, but there was a little more to it than that. Early in the meeting I had preached on the return of Christ and had taken a swipe at the pre-millennial view, calling myself a "pan-millennialist." (Everything will pan out in the end.) During our Bible talks at his house I realized he was doing his best to convince me of his pre-millennial position, which he was never able to do. When the meeting was over and I was preparing to leave he said, "Brother Hall, I believe God's grace is so great He will save you in spite of your ignorance." I sure hope so, Brother Clarke. I sure hope so.

May 24-30, 1958 - Plum Run church, Rayland, OH

This meeting was special because it was the first revival I had ever conducted. I was 22 years old. Why they called me I'll never understand. I was shy, didn't know the Word, had no experience, and stumbled for words when I preached. I screamed and spat and got all red in the face. There were no additions during this meeting except one great addition for me. The song leader was a pretty, blue eyed girl from down the road about five miles named Patsy Lee McBee. There's no way my preaching impressed her and I had no money. It had to be my good looks.

June 10-23, 1964 Harrison church of Christ-Johnson City, TN

This church on the north side of Johnson City had just asked their minister to leave and he had sixty days to close out his ministry. He had already accepted another ministry in Indiana. I offered to cancel the revival until their new minister came but he said, "Louis, I would like to close out my ministry here on a good note. We have many people ready to accept Christ and the church really needs reviving." We selected a theme for the meeting of "Bearing His Cross," and the church really got behind the effort. They had a week of intense, door to door visitation and ran ads in the paper and on the radio. The last night of the meeting 220 were in attendance. During the two weeks seventy-five people responded to the invitation. Thirty-five came to confess Christ and be immersed and forty others came to transfer membership, rededicate their lives to Christ, or give themselves to evangelism. This meeting was the talk of the town. To date this was the largest number of people I have seen come to Christ in any American revival I've conducted. This church went on to see greater days as the years went by.

October 8-22, 1962  Church of Christ- Hopedale, OH

 I was more than thrilled when Patsy's home church invited me to come and preach a two week revival in the fall of 1962. The preacher Clarence (Rusty) Morris had married us just three years before, and we loved him dearly. We drove from our home in the Tennessee hills to Ohio and stayed with Patsy's mom and dad on their farm just a few miles from Hopedale. Doug was two and Tammy was four months old. During these two weeks Rusty and I visited daily in homes throughout the village and in the surrounding area. Large crowds attended every night of the meeting and ten persons came to confess Christ and be baptized. One of those who responded was Glen Christy. In time Glen would grow so in Christ that he would become an elder and Sunday school teacher and serve for many years. Though having stepped down recently so younger men could serve, Glen is still faithful, along with his wife Doris, and both are dear friends of ours.

 We were honored and blessed by being in the home of Frank and Margaret Gregory during that meeting. Both are of Italian descent. They had been "good Catholics" and were baptized after hearing an old friend of mine, Leland Tyrrel, preach. Frank had a singing voice as sweet and clear as Dean Martin, who grew up just a few miles away. When Doug was just a small boy he heard Dean Martin singing on the radio and said, "Hey Dad, listen to Dean Martin trying to sing like Frank Gregory." Margaret could prepare those great Italian dishes that just couldn't be topped. I remember thinking how pretty she was then and she's as pretty today. They became instant friends and the bond between us has only grown through the years. All three of our children loved and admired them and still do. They have had a tremendous influence on us and our ministry. Though they are getting along in years, Margaret is still cooking and Frank is still singing and they are still faithful to Christ and His church.

October 4-11, 1964 church of Christ-Smith Hill, OH

 We concluded a great two week meeting at West Union,

Ohio and Patsy's mom and dad met us at Hillsboro where Patsy and the children went with them to spend a week on the farm at Smithfield. I continued on to Smith Hill, Ohio for another week of revival. I arrived at this little country church about 5:00PM and entered the church house and rested until the people began to arrive around 6:30PM. I had never been here and did not know anyone or where I'd be staying that week. As the people arrived they were friendly and humble people and welcomed me sincerely. After a short song service one of the elders introduced me (they were without a minister at the time) and I walked to the big, solid oak pulpit to preach. It was then that I saw it for the first time - in the center of the pulpit was an engraved brass plate which read, "SIR, WE WOULD SEE JESUS". This verse is found in John 12:21. It was a stark reminder that this small group of farmers had not come to see me. They wanted to see and hear Jesus. I think of this each time I step up to preach. We have something far greater than ourselves to preach. I did my best to share the message of the cross with those humble people that week and seven confessed Christ and obeyed him in baptism.

One night early in the week a man about forty years old approached me, and using a small pad he asked if I could come to his house the next day and teach him and his wife. They were both deaf mutes. They had met in a school for deaf mutes and married soon after. I tossed and turned that night wondering how I would go about this. When I arrived at their house the next day they had set up a blackboard for my use. They were both excellent at reading lips so communication was not all that difficult. I had grown up with a friend named Mike Hall who was deaf but great at lip reading. After about an hour of looking at scripture, writing on the board, and them reading my lips, both of them went to the board and in turn wrote, "I believe Jesus Christ is the Son of God." At the meeting that night both were buried with Christ in baptism. When the meeting closed I packed my car and headed to the next meeting singing praises to God for what He had done at Smith Hill.

Crooked Creek church of Christ- Peach Creek WV

    I couldn't even begin to remember the number of times I have gone to these beautiful hills to preach. The first was shortly after a devastating flood hit the area after a mine dam burst in February 1972. It killed 125, injured more than 1100, and left more than 4000 homeless. Property damage was more than $50 million. Though Crooked Creek was out of the path of this flood, almost everyone knew someone affected by it and several had friends and relatives there.

    I loved these humble people the first time I preached there, and they have been like family since. We always stay with Bob and Donna Miller and their beautiful daughter, Tia. We dubbed their home, "The Miller Motel", but it's nothing at all like a motel. It's a happy home where God's servants are so welcome and always made to feel so. After a week here we leave feeling rested and refreshed.

    The preaching of truth is always well received and God has given some wonderful victories in meetings there. Good friend Pete Parsons was a Vietnam veteran when I met him. During the revival he obeyed the Lord and has remained faithful all these years. John Bennett, a lawyer and now Logan County's prosecuting attorney, heard the good news and obeyed it. He is one of the elders there now.

    A visit to Crooked Creek is never complete without a visit to the home of Howard McNeely. Howard was only 19 when Japan bombed Pearl Harbor in 1941. He crossed the English Channel 23 times as a tail gunner on a B-17. On the 24$^{th}$ mission they went into the water. Rescued, he returned home a hero with a purple heart. Howard is a humble man and loves the Lord. I count it a tremendous blessing to know him.

Mt Carmel Christian near Irvine, KY

    Not far from Hanging Rock in Estil County Kentucky is another favorite place to preach. For the past eight years or so I have been going there every September to conduct revival. Even as I complete this book, I am scheduled to return this fall. On my first visit there I became lost and showed up at this church on the mountain about fifteen minutes late. When I finally arrived and walked in the minister, Butch, announced, "You must be Lou Hall. We thought you must have stopped off down at the boot legging joint."

They are just down to earth Kentucky people who love to sing praises to God and hear Bible preaching. God has given us some really wonderful victories in meetings. Once I was visiting with one of the elders and we called on a man who was not a Christian. He agreed to let us talk to him about his need for Christ. As we began to talk, he began to cry and said, "I'm sorry, men." The elder put his hand on the man's shoulder and said, "Don't be ashamed to cry. I'll cry with you." And he did. That very day we went to the church building and baptized him into Christ. The folks at Mt Carmel love the Lord and we know they love us also. They are faithful in supporting our mission work with their finances and prayer.

## Mudfork church of Christ, Bluefield, VA

One of the first churches I preached revival for more than 40 years ago was Mudfork. I have been back time after time. Located in some rugged but beautiful mountains, they are only a few miles from the West Virginia line. A Craig County, Virginia boy has been their minister since I've known the church. Johnnie Elmore is a nephew to one of our great restoration leaders, R.E. Elmore and an able preacher in his own right.

When I first began going there for revivals they were always two weeks long. It wasn't at all uncommon to see ten or more people obey the Gospel. We always spent the afternoons out in the community visiting from house to house. Crowds were always large and visiting churches helped swell the attendance.

Aside from all the victory and great fellowship, I remember two funny things that happened there during revival. We were to end the meeting on Sunday with Homecoming and dinner on the grounds. I began to announce during the week that I planned to "make" a cake for the meal. On Saturday I took a box, put a few rocks in it and iced it over with chocolate icing. It was beautiful, and at the meal I asked Uncle Charlie Bowman to slice it. This brother was a genuine, no nonsense Christian and when he realized what I'd done, he "laid hands on me." He exclaimed, "Shame on you for wasting that icing. I ought to make you eat box, rocks, and all."

The other incident was when word came to us that if the visiting preacher called on a certain man in the community, he planned to whip him. I weighed 245 pounds at the time and couldn't understand why he would want to whip me, and probably doubted that he could. Before the meeting ended I finally went to his home. His wife answered the door and told me he was around back. I walked around the house and here stood an older man with only one leg. I never laughed but I wanted to at the thought of him whipping me. I now knew he couldn't because he couldn't catch me. We had a great visit that afternoon.

Mudfork is a great place to preach and it's always a joy to be there.They are blessed to have elders who can preach and teach and do so. They are also the longest supporting church since we became involved in missions.

## Tannersville church of Christ in Virginia

Another congregation in the heart of beautiful Virginia mountains is located not far from Hungry Mother State park in the highlands of Virginia. The membership is small but the faith of the members is large. Don't dare come here with anything more or less than the Bible. I've gone there so long and so often that I've watched the children grow from infants to college students. Many precious and dear people who had the vision to establish this church after the New Testament have gone on to be with the Lord.

One night during my many revivals there a lady said, "Louis, see that woman over there? I wish you would go talk with her this week. She's not a Christian." The next day Patsy and I drove up a breathtaking valley and found her house. As we approached the house I called out and her mother came to the porch. I asked if Mary was home and she said she would get her. As she came out on the porch, I wasn't prepared for what she said. She said, "I'm Mary. I'm the sinner." There on that humble porch I taught her the Bible and God's plan for redeeming man and that night at the meeting she was baptized into Christ. It's always such a delight to see her when I return to Tannersville.

While at Tannersville we usually stay with Joe and Wanda Holmes and their children, Steven, Sasha and Angela. We've watched them grow from infants to adults and we love them like we love our own grandchildren.

I could continue almost endlessly about evangelistic and revival meetings we conducted and continue to conduct. Once this book is printed I'll undoubtedly think of many I should have mentioned. Not all churches have them anymore and the great numbers of souls saved are seldom seen in America like we saw in those early days. There are probably a lot of reasons for this and not all of them bad. It's a good thing that people come to Christ in our churches throughout the year and not just at a special time. But whether you call it revival or not, I can't imagine the time could ever come when it won't be beneficial to gather our people together and rally them to the cross. We live in a day when we are blessed with some great Bible preachers. Why not invite them in to speak and encourage our people? I had a hard time understanding that our people sometimes get tired of hearing us just as we sometimes get tired of preaching to them. A different voice and personality saying the same things we've been saying could make a big difference.

## FLYING HIGH

So our first year was wonderful to us and I began 1975 with much faith and optimism. Invitations to conduct revival and evangelistic meetings continued to come in and I was kept busy in many good meetings. I would speak in four of our bible colleges that year: Cincinnati Bible Seminary, Kentucky Christian College, Bluefield College of Evangelism, and Roanoke Bible College. At Kentucky I taught a class on Mission Methods and spoke for a three night Faith Promise Renewal. I would also make another trip to Southeast Asia. This time my brother Russell and his brother-in-law Norman Ward accompanied me. It was my third trip there and how wonderful it was to visit some of the same places and people again. I continued to be moved by the great need in this part of the world and was glad to be such a small part in encouraging national workers and now some American missionaries who were starting to move into Thailand. Paul Fuller had gone there from Cincinnati to teach in the bible college and had set up a ham radio station. Early one morning I was able to talk with my son, Douglas back in North Carolina. It greatly impressed me, but it would be almost forty years before I would have a need for this and set up my own station in the Caribbean.

Patsy and the children were busy as the kids progressed in school. The girls were in band and Doug played football and headed up the Photography club at school. Patsy was working as a Nurse at Morehead Hospital.

1976 would bring about some changes that would effect me for the rest of my life. Since I was a small child I had possessed a passion for flying. At age ten or eleven I would stand at the edge of a grass strip near home and watch the small Piper Cubs take off and land. I have a beautiful painting of that little airport, painted by my talented friend Barbara Sanders, hanging on the wall of my office today. World War 2 had ended and there was a surge in general aviation. I would clutch the barbed wire surrounding the airport and wish someone would offer me a ride. No one ever did. I remember the day I promised myself that one day I would fly and own my own plane and take any little boy or girl who wanted one on an airplane ride. I kept that promise.

I had taken a few lessons in Johnson City, TN in 1963 but due to lack of funds had dropped out of the flight program at Appalachian Flying Service. I resumed it again in 1971 but the same thing happened. In 1972 I again started and managed to solo after about seven hours of instruction. I was flying out of Warf airport in Reidsville, NC. This was a small airport that was opened in 1946 by Henry Warf. The sod runway was only 2000 ft. long. On one end there were 100 foot tall trees and high voltage power lines. On the other end was a lake. I always took off toward the lake thinking I would be better off putting it into the lake rather than the wires and trees. I learned the key to flying out of Warf field was to get as far back as I could, hold the brakes, push the throttle all way in, pull back all way on the yoke and release the brakes. By the time I was screaming three quarters down the strip I was airborne. I didn't know then that this was how missionaries got in and out of short strips on the mission fields. I never put the little Cessna 150 in the lake but one of Henry's other students did. In March of 1972 my instructor had a series of medical problems and I once again set aside my dream of flying, promising to resume it when I could. For the next four years I did no flying, though I did think a lot about it.

On July 8, 1976 I went to my old home to visit with Mom and Dad. Dad had been in the Hospital and was now home. I remember telling him I was leaving that day for Ohio to perform a wedding and would be back to see him shortly. I had no idea this would be my last time to see him in this life. The phone rang sometime in the early morning hours of July 10 in Ohio and no one had to tell me what it was. My Dad had slipped away from his body of pain and quietly gone to be with Jesus. Clyde H. Hall had been born January 9, 1904 in Floyd County, Virginia. He had worked as a farmer, logger, a rivet man in the shipyards during the war, and for the majority of his life in the cotton mill at Draper. As far back as I can remember Dad had a problem with the demon alcohol. He would go long periods when he wouldn't drink but suddenly he would began again. It was a grievous thing for Mom and all of us kids. When he was sober he was good as gold but when drinking you just never knew. One night years later Mom told me the story of why Dad might have been addicted to drink. In 1939 when I was only four, he had gone to a tent revival, interested in making a change in his life. At the close of each service the preacher would encourage the sinners to come, kneel at an altar, and "pray through," whatever that meant. He went forward every night but felt nothing. On the last night he was told that evidently he had committed the unpardonable sin and could never be forgiven. After that he never had any interest in the things of God and his drinking got worse. I often wonder what a difference it would have made over all those years if someone had sat down with an open Bible and taught him the way of the Lord. That did happen in 1951 when Roy Miller taught him and led him to Christ. Dad went on to be a Sunday school teacher and an elder.

When I remember Clyde Hall today I don't remember a man given to drink or foul language. I see him poring over his Bible late at night or giving thanks at the communion table. I see him teaching a Bible class or out in the community inviting others to church. I remember a man who was faithful unto death.

In late 1976 my brother Russell would resign his ministry in Roanoke, VA to work with Southeast Asia Mission also. Since his trip there in 1975 this had been playing on his mind. He and his wife Glenda were great additions to the Mission, and the greatest thing to come from this is that they would go on to establish their own mission in Cambodia. They have worked with orphaned children in Cambodia for many years now and continue to do a great work there. Russ is my brother and my friend and I thank God for the work they continue to do.

In the spring of 1975 a new airport opened just five miles from our house. Rockingham County airport at Shiloh is a modern facility. It has beautiful paved runways that are five thousand feet long. It also has lights and instrument landing capabilities. It has Piper aircraft for rent, and the planes from Shiloh flying over my house soon gave me the fever. In January

1977 I began flying again and on Feb.22 I received my private pilot certification. In the weeks that followed I have entries in my log book of great numbers of people I took flying who had never been in a plane. The oldest was 82 and the youngest 6.

In May of that year, two of my brothers, a brother-in-law, and I bought our own plane. It was a beautiful four-passenger Cessna 172. It was a piece of cake to fly in and out of that long runway after flying at Warf's postage stamp. I used it in revivals in Kentucky and eastern North Carolina as well as others cities in Virginia and North Carolina. The kids loved it, and Doug would solo it when he was only 17 year old. He only had seven hours instruction when he soloed. You think it's tough to hand a 17 year old the car keys and watch them drive away? Try handing them the keys to your airplane and watch them take to the wild blue yonder.

In time the others lost interest, and one by one I bought their part, thus becoming the sole owner of N2403U. In the first year I logged more than 50 hours in "zero-three-uniform," a good bit in the Lord's work but most of it just for pleasure. I had many funny experiences and a few pretty serious ones in the years I owned it.

One beautiful October morning I drove to the airport prepared to fly to Roanoke Rapids, NC for a week of preaching. When I arrived at the airport there were a number of people sitting on the fence or at picnic tables watching planes fly in and out. I walked to the plane with my suitcase and a few other items and loaded them into the back. Then I began, as I always did, to carefully pre-flight the plane. I checked the oil, kicked the tires, and did all the things we're taught to do before we take to the skies. I then untied the wings, removed the chocks from the wheels, and climbed in. Once inside I clicked my seatbelt, picked up the clipboard, and began the check list for flight. I cracked open the throttle, gave it a few shots of primer, turned on the master switch and the ignition key, cracked the window, and called out, "Clear!" When I engaged the starter the engine roared to life. I allowed it to warm a minute then I spoke into the radio microphone and announced I was ready to taxi to the active runway. The base operator answered back saying the active runway was 31 and there was light traffic. I placed the mic back in its holder and began to ease the throttle in, but nothing happened. I gave it more power, but I was not moving. I couldn't imagine what was wrong with the plane. Then I looked toward the fence and picnic tables and the spectators were pointing and roaring with laughter. With a red face I shut the engine down, climbed out of the plane, and untied the tail. After that I was glad to disappear into the sky.

  I announced to Patsy one morning that I was going to Elizabeth City, NC to visit our our granddaughter Lynn who was just a little tyke at the time. She almost shouted, "Well, I'm going with you!" I said, "Well, I'm flying down." Eyes wide she said, "Oh?" She has never enjoyed flying and especially not in a small plane. But grandchildren can do strange things to grandparents, and after thinking a minute she said, "O.K." Before I knew it she had invited our granddaughter's other grandmother, Dottie Hand from across the street to go along. As I taxied down the runway I was aware that I couldn't "cowboy" it today. I had to fly like a professional with these two pretty ladies aboard. So I gently flew it out of the airport and did everything smoothly and by the book. As I turned left out of the pattern and pulled back on the yoke to reach altitude, suddenly both doors on the plane popped open and we were looking down into the tops of trees. As calmly as I could I shut both doors and locked them and we proceeded to Elizabeth City. About 15 miles out I called the airport and was given the active runway and traffic report. I opted to fly a straight in approach on runway 10 and began my descent at 1500 feet. This runway was 7,219 feet long and it seemed our approach took forever. I was carefully watching two huge HC-130's flying east of the field and began setting up for the landing when Patsy asked, "Are we landing there?" "Of course," I replied,"where else?" She not so calmly said, "You're landing on the taxi way." I quickly turned the plane to the left and set it down on the center line of runway 10. I then calmly said, "Just wanted to see if you knew the difference."

My brother Butch and I left early one morning on a flight to South Boston, VA. It was a bright, clear morning with not a cloud in sight. Butch was flying that morning and I sat in right seat with a cup of coffee and the latest *Flying* magazine. We chatted along the way and I drank my coffee and looked over the magazine, scarcely looking at the earth below. Finally I heard him call South Boston to get the runway information and latest traffic. He began descending to land, and it was then I noticed something wrong. I said, "Butch, we're not at South Boston." He replied, "Oh yes we are. Didn't you hear him clear me to land?" I said, "Butch, if we're at South Boston they have torn down the race track and planted a forest of big oak trees where it stood and they have also built a restaurant on the field." Surprised, he said, "We're not at South Boston! Wonder where we are?" By then he was 50 feet above the runway so we landed. We parked the airplane and stepped inside the restaurant, still having no clue where we were. We ordered coffee and the waitress asked, "You boys lost?" I replied, "Well, maybe a little. Where are we?" She said, "I heard you call in over the radio and then I saw you landing here. You're in Chase City, VA." We laughed about this for years and neither of us took the blame for being off course eight miles. We were sure the plane's compass was out of whack.

On a more serious note, I flew 03U to to Belhaven, NC one August morning to preach seven days for Mt Olive church of Christ. The nearest airport was in Washington about an hour away, so I landed in a pasture field just a short distance from the church building. Several mornings during that week I flew out over the Outer Banks. I landed at Kitty Hawk, just a short walk from where the Wright brothers became "first in flight." I flew down to Cape Hatteras and circled that beautiful lighthouse. This was exciting in that those I took with me had never flown before, and to see the "Graveyard of the Atlantic" was priceless. After a good week of revival I loaded the plane and planned to depart early on Saturday morning. I woke up Saturday morning, and looking out I saw a heavy mist. When I got to the plane it was still quite misty with poor visibility, and I had to wait almost two hours for it to burn off. Finally it lifted enough for me to fly and I was on my way home. I didn't want to leave this late because thunder storms would build up in the afternoon and I sure didn't want to tangle with one of these. I knew I only had a half tank of fuel in both left and right tanks. I always made it a practice of topping off the tank every time I parked it but there was no fuel available in the pasture field. My plan was to stop at Danville, VA and fill the tanks. I probably had enough to get me home but there was no need to take that chance. Things went well the first hour and then I began to see huge thunder heads on the horizon. Being inexperienced as I was I should have found a small airport and landed, but wanting to get home I did what I knew not to do. I tried to fly around the thunder heads and before I realized it I was in it. It was a wild ride. I was so frightened that I almost quit flying the plane without realizing it. The stall warning came on several times and jolted me back to reality. I remember telling God that if He would get me back on the ground I'd give up this stupid love of flying. I've learned since that most pilots pray that sometime in their life. I was grateful for what little instrument training I had received. I was not instrument-rated but here I was flying strictly on instruments. I was trying desperately to fly out of this storm, and it seemed to be getting worse. I would be lifted to four thousand feet and suddenly drop to three. I watched the fuel in the left tank drop to empty and I switched to the right tank. It had about a fourth of tank and when this was gone, it would be over for me. Finally I tuned the radio to 122.1 and spoke into the mic. "Greensboro approach, this is Cessna 03U." When the controller came back to me I told him what was happening. I was a low-time private pilot without an instrument rating and I had flown into instrument conditions. There would surely be a penalty for this. I might even have my license suspended for a period of time. He gave me a couple of small turns to make since I had no transponder and quickly identified me on his scope. He then told me to descend to two thousand feet and he also gave me a heading to fly. In a very short time I broke out of the clouds and there just ahead of me was the Danville airport. Nothing had ever looked so beautiful to me. When I parked the plane a young boy came out to top off the tanks. I went inside, hoping no one was in the bathroom. My legs were like rubber. I thanked God repeatedly. I got coffee out of a machine and I shook so badly I couldn't drink it. It took more than an hour for me to become calm and collected enough to fly the short leg on home. The sun was starting to set and the sky was beautiful as I flew west into the sunset and landed at Shiloh. I told Patsy I had a little problem coming home but it all worked out OK. That night when we all settled down, I lay awake unable to sleep. About midnight I got up and quietly slipped out of the house. I drove the five miles back to the airport. It was dark. Not a soul was around. I unlocked the plane and climbed inside. I pushed the seat all way back and leaning back I fell fast asleep. Before I fell asleep I thanked God again and said, "And God, about that promise I made up there this afternoon, do you think we could .. uh?"

Above: Flight training
Below: Cessna 172, N2403U

105

## ANOTHER CHANGE OF DIRECTION

In September of 1977 I traveled to Jennings, LA to conduct revival services. This was cajun country and a delightful place to visit. I had been there for two other meetings, so I knew many of the people. I loved their food and friendliness. A few nights into the meeting a tall, well-dressed gentleman, wearing western boots and suit introduced himself to me. His name was Hollins Duhon of Baton Rouge. I didn't dream it at the time but for the next sixteen years he would have a tremendous influence on my life and ministry. Born in 1915 of French Arcadian parents, he grew up in the Catholic church and was in fact being groomed to become a Priest. Before reaching adulthood he met brother Everest Hebert (pronounced "eh-bear") who had read and reasoned his way out of the Catholic church and became a "Christian only." Hebert was a huge man of around 300 pounds when I met him in 1963, and he became a powerful preacher and defender of the faith. As a result of his preaching of the Bible thousands of Catholics in Southwest Louisiana heard the truth for the first time and embraced it. Churches of Christ sprang up throughout that whole area. One of those who heard and obeyed was this young future priest, Hollins Duhon. Herbert taught Hollins and other young men the Bible. They would meet with him each day after school in what was dubbed, "The school of the prophets." Quite a few of these young men would go on to become preachers of the Gospel, and Hollins was one of them. He also had his eye on Herbert's daughter, Marie and later married her. Fluent in French and English, brother Hollins was in demand as an evangelist, especially in Louisiana and Texas. He never went to college but was so well educated and talented that he was once offered the presidency of Dallas Christian College. He declined this invitation because of his love for preaching.

The night Hollins introduced himself to me he went on to say that he had recently started doing mission work in Haiti and had come back home to see if he could find someone to come help him. My immediate reply was that I was busy as could be and, anyway I didn't know anything about Haiti or hardly where it was. He then asked where I was staying while in Louisana and I told him the Airport Motel. He asked if he could stop by and talk more with me about it. I said I saw no point in talking more about it since I knew I couldn't help him. He said, "Well, I need prayer for this mission. Could I stop by and have you pray for me?" Checkmate. He had me, and the next morning bright and early he was knocking on my door. His favorite posture for prayer was on his knees and for a long time we prayed together on our knees about the work in Haiti. Before he left the motel I had agreed to come down for two weeks in November to preach and teach and see the work. Before he drove away he said, "And if you know anyone with any medical training, try to bring them with you." I thought how amazing this was since I was married to a great nurse and he could not have possibly known this. Later in the day I remembered I had mentioned in my sermon the night before that Patsy was a nurse. I went to the library later in the day and looked at a world map to see where Haiti was.

In early November Patsy and I flew Eastern airlines to Miami and then into Port au Prince, Haiti. She had asked me to promise her two things before we left. The first was that we would spend the night in Port au Prince and make the five hour trip to Dessalines the next day. Being her first trip out of the country, she wanted to acclimate gradually to things and didn't want to travel overland at night. The second was that I would not leave her alone and take off preaching somewhere after we arrived. I am ashamed to say that I broke both promises within 24 hours. Hollins was waiting at the airport and after a long time clearing customs, he said, "Let's go." We piled our bags in this old beat-up Ford pickup and away we went. It would be close to midnight when we would finally arrive in the villiage of Dessalines in the Artibonite valley. Here I've asked Patsy to describe what she felt as we made our first trip into the back country of Haiti.

*"We arrived in Port au Prince late in the evening. The weather in NC was cold when we left earlier that day. When we*

*got off the plane in PAP the heat was stifling. We had to go through security and customs before we could leave the airport. Customs opened all our bags and went through everything we had. When we were finally cleared we met Hollins who was waiting for us just outside security. Before we left the states I had asked Louis if he would promise me two things. The first was that we would spend the night in PAP before leaving for the five hour trip to Dessalines. The second was that he would not leave me somewhere alone.*

*Hollins was so happy to see us. We were tired after traveling since early morning. We loaded our bags in back of the Ford truck, climbed in, and began the long trip to Dessalines. So much for spending the night in PAP. It was a very dark night and I had no idea what was out beyond the headlights of the truck. Since there was no air conditioning we rode with the windows down. The smells of Haiti assailed our nostrils as we rode along the road, fields, and villages on the way. Even today when I smell diesel fuel or burning trash or leaves I always remember Haiti.*

*Hollins had so much to tell us so he talked as he drove and had to look at you when he talked. I sat in the middle between Louis and Hollins and held on to Louis's leg all the way. Somewhere along the way we came upon a dead horse in the road but Hollins was so busy talking he never saw it. I put on the brakes to no avail. He ran over the horse and never realized it. We laughed later saying we hoped no one was riding the horse. The road was so rough with potholes and broken pavement that it made little difference if you hit something or dropped into a pothole.*

*We finally arrived in Dessalines sometime around midnight. It was quite dark with no electricity in this village of thousands. We could see small fires burning as we looked out into the darkness. Even at midnight it was still very hot. After the long trip I had to go to the bathroom so asked where it was. Hollins replied that it was "out back" so I took my flashlight and went "out back." I found a little shed with a hole in the seat and cracks in the door. Due to the cracks in the door I turned off my light after I went inside. Big mistake! It was so dark! I turned my light on again and there were large roaches crawling up and down the door right in front of me. I burst through the door yelling for Louis.*

*Early the next morning after a restless night we loaded the truck with some medical supplies and a wonderful Haitian man named Leon Decade. Brother Decade would be my helper and interpreter. We then went to another village not too far from Dessalines. Here Louis and Hollins dropped me off to do medical work and they left to preach somewhere. The second promise had been broken. This was my first trip out of the U.S. and I knew nothing of the dangers I might face. Haiti is a very poor and undeveloped country but the people were gracious and friendly. Though I did not speak Creole we seemed to find a way to communicate. We would learn so much from the Christians in this poor and struggling country over the next sixteen years."*

Our two weeks in Haiti passed quickly as we kept busy preaching, teaching, and conducting medical clinics in this valley of more than 100,000 people. The night before we left for the airport for our return flight home, I shook Hollins' hand and told him we would come and work with him on the field and do public relations for the work when we were in the states. He said, "God bless you, brother Hall." and then gave me a giant hug. Our decision to work in Haiti had as much to do with him as it did the great need we saw there. To this day I have never met a man more gentle or servant like than Hollins Duhon. It was his great delight to serve others, and their station in life made no difference to him. You were not with him two minutes until you knew to whom he belonged and that his sole purpose in life was serving God. This man of God rubbed off on me, and I'll always believe I'm a better servant for having known him.

## CHANGING COURSE

Upon returning home I announced our decision to leave South East Asia Mission and work with Dessalines Christian Development in Haiti. Russell was now working full time with SEAM so there would be no shortage of someone to speak on their behalf. My revival schedule would be the same and my PR work would now be for the work in Haiti rather than S.E. Asia. We never missed a beat and 1978 filled fast. I made sure to leave plenty of weeks for working in Haiti, and since it was so close I could go more often and spend longer periods of time on the field. It was also the ideal place for Patsy to do medical work and teach women and children. In January we enrolled in French class at Rockingham Community College. On the first day of class we were the first ones there and grabbed a seat at the front of the room. With book and notebook in hand we were ready to learn French. Soon a young girl came in wearing a very short skirt and popping bubble gum. She jumped up on the teacher's desk and began to swing her legs back and forth. I whispered to Patsy, "Just wait till the teacher arrives. She will be surprised." I got the surprise since she *was* the teacher!

I presented the great need in Haiti to several churches in the next two months and was able to generate a lot of interest and some regular support. The first church wanting to send a team to help construct a church building was Faith church of Christ in Burlington, IN. Later they would send some great men down to help us for two weeks. This would be the beginning of many churches sending hundreds of people to help in the work over a period of sixteen years. These teams came mostly from churches that gladly supported this work with prayer and finances. This work could have never been the great success it was without their help.

It's not easy for me to describe Haiti in just a few paragraphs. By far the poorest country in the Western hemisphere, it has not improved much in all the years since we went there. Constantly in political turmoil, we went through three overthrows of the government in the years we lived and worked there. Seldom did the children in our school complete an entire year without violence disrupting their study. It was not unusual to start to the city only to be turned back because the road was blocked or fighting was taking place somewhere along the way. The nearest city to us was Goniaves, about an hour away. One day I drove in to get a block of ice, and as I entered the city there was an erie calm. No one was on the streets except soldiers, and machine guns were set up on every corner. I purchased the ice, climbed in my truck, and made my way out of town. I have American newspaper clippings saved for me that tell of a blood bath in Goniaves that night when soldiers clashed with citizens protesting the government. Many were killed.

The people of Haiti are of African decent, having been brought to the island as slaves by the French in the 1600s. Haiti, which means "land of high mountains" occupies the Western side of the island of Hispaniola. The other half is the Dominican Republic. Haiti's land area is some 10,750 square miles. Its highest peak is 8793 feet. The official language is French and Creole, though it's usually pretty easy to find someone who speaks English. Its religion is predominately Roman Catholic but in reality it is a Voodoo/Catholic mix. The Catholic church tried to fight Voodoo in its early days but finally gave in and accepted it. We knew people who would attend Mass in the morning and their voodoo devil worship at night. After a slave revolt Haiti declared their independence from France in 1804 and became the first independent black nation in the Americas. The story is often told in Haiti that when the slave revolt brought them independence the new leaders dedicated the new nation to Satan. I've heard politicians and people in America deny this, but in sixteen years in Haiti I never heard one Haitian deny it. It's an established fact and in my opinion the number one reason this country has never been blessed. When we went to Haiti in 1977 the population was six and one half million. In 2011 it was nine and one half million.

In 1957, minister of health and labor, François Duvalier (Papa Doc) was elected President. He ruled Haiti and terrorized the people with a group of henchmen known as *Tonton Macutes*. (More about them later) He would declare himself *président à vie* (president for life) in 1963. I vividly remember talking to old people who remembered him well. One story I heard often was that he would show up in a village, take some woman's baby, throw it into the air and catch it on his bayonet, and drink the blood. He was an avowed worshiper of Satan. When he suspected someone was his enemy he would have them imprisoned and torture them in various ways. One of his favorites was to have them submerged in acid while he watched them die. He is estimated to have killed as many as 30,000 of his own people during his reign. Once when a bomb exploded near his palace he had 19 of his soldiers shot. When President Kennedy was assassinated Papa Doc proudly took credit for his death saying he had placed a voodoo curse on him. He hated the United States and all white people and at the same time greedily took the many millions of U.S. dollars our gullible political leaders sent to him. Haiti was relieved of this man's curse when he died of a heart attack in early 1971. Before he died he appointed his 19 year old son, Jean Claude (Baby Doc) his successor.

    Having first visited Haiti in 1977, I returned to work with brother Hollins Duhon in March 1978. Things were rather quiet at this time. The country was under the leadership of President Jean-Claude Duvalier. (Baby Doc ) These next couple of years were some of the most peaceful in Haiti's long history. No one knew if Jean-Claude Duvalier would be as ruthless as his daddy. Some reports say he was, but he was happy to turn over much of his power to his mother and other family members while he enjoyed being a playboy. He married in 1980, spending three million dollars on the wedding. This would be the beginning of his undoing.  The one and only time I saw him he was riding a new Harley Davidson motorcycle and throwing quarters to the poor children on the streets of Port au Prince. In 1984 a U.S. Ambassador to Haiti wrote, "It can honestly be said that under Baby Doc's rule Haiti has enjoyed it's longest period of violence-free stability." But in 1985 there would be widespread rioting in the streets. It would start near us in Gonaives, Haiti's fourth largest city.

Brother Duhon had visited Haiti several years before moving there when he traveled with evangelist Reggie Thomas of White Fields out of Joplin, MO. Being fluent in French he was a hit with the people wherever he spoke. While he preached in the out-of-the-way town of Dessalines he drew such large crowds that the mayor came out to see what was happening. He liked what he heard and promised 10 acres of land at the entrance of the city if Hollins would come back and develop it as a Christian development. This is what Hollins had presented to me in the motel at Jennings, LA in the summer of 1977. On this land would be a multi-purpose church building which would provide seating for 500. It would contain two full-size apartments with bath facilities and a kitchen. A Christian school would be established with eight classrooms to begin with and more to be added. A small medical clinic would be established. Patients would be seen free of charge and no one would be turned away. Doctors and dentists from the U.S. were asked to come and help out, and many did. A feeding program would be instituted so hungry children could get at least one meal per day. Two deep wells would be drilled so the people could get safe water and not have to walk miles for the polluted water they were drinking. Space would be provided for a community garden so the people could grow their own vegetables. Over our sixteen year involvement we saw all of this and more become a reality.

As we began working locally in Dessalines we made sometimes daily trips to a large spring of water on the edge of town for baptismal services. It was here the women washed their clothes. Many saw a baptism who had never seen one. It was also one of the greatest places to teach or learn and we used it for both. As souls obeyed the gospel the church began to grow and soon we had outgrown the small pole barn we were using. Several hours each day were spent in construction as we worked to complete the first church house. By the time it was completed we had more than one hundred attending.

A great factor in the growth of churches from Dessalines to the Dominican border was our quarterly seminars. We would send messages to churches in these outlying areas of Haiti announcing a leadership seminar. Food and lodging would be provided but they would have to provide their own transportation. They came in great numbers from every direction and all denominations. We fed them rice and beans, and they camped on the ground or in the church building. We had sessions from 9 AM until around 4 PM and preaching services at 7 PM. It was a wonderful idea and became so popular that we had men walk fifteen miles across the mountains to attend. Often a man would bring his wife and children. Once one of our most aspiring young preachers, a 23 year old from Circa in the mountains near Dominican Republic was on his way to our seminar. He was to be one of our speakers, but the bus he was riding ran off the mountain near Cape Haitien and he was killed instantly. The seminar began on a sad note when this was announced. We'll never know the good these seminars accomplished. Entire denominations became Christians only and preachers of the Gospel were trained in the word. All of our classes were Bible classes except the one I taught on personal evangelism. I soon learned they knew that subject better than I did, and they were far less hesitant to speak to someone about Christ than I was.

Dessalines was a city of about 60,000 when we went there. It had no electricity or phones. We used a small Honda generator to run our electric saws and tools during construction. The streets were not paved and no modern conveniences were available. It now has a population of over 100,000 with 24-hour electrical service and telephone lines. It had once been the capital of Haiti, the only black capital in the world. Named after their great warrior, J.J. Dessalines, it was said that he loved this city greatly.

Though we were living and evangelizing in Dessalines we did our best to reach out into the areas of the Artibonite river valley. Usually about one night a week we would hold a crusade in one of several places within an hour or so from where we lived. In time we were able to establish a church in these places and a team from America would then come and build a building for them. We had been trying to find a night to preach in the village of Neil, north of Dessalines but every evening it would began raining and the roads would be so muddy we couldn't make the trip. Finally we had about three days with no rain and the road had dried enough for us to go. I told Patsy to get ready for the trip into this back country. We loaded the truck with some of our own people to lead singing. Mrs. Margie Burks of Rosedale, VA and one of her friends were visiting us. I was glad they were there to see first hand what we were doing. We arrived at Neil and within thirty minutes more than two hundred had gathered for the meeting. After about 45 minutes of singing I stood up to preach and the rain began to fall. I told Patsy to head for the truck because if we were stuck here in the rain it might be days before we could get out. As the people also began leaving, I noticed one of our old men down on his knees praying. Suddenly the rain stopped and every star in the sky seemed to appear. The departing crowd sighed aloud and quickly returned to the cleared area. I preached on the return of Christ and 26 people came to confess Christ as Lord. We baptized them in a nearby canal that night and the Lord's church at Neil was born. On the way home I asked the old gentleman if he was praying for the rain to stop. He said, "Yes, brother Hall." I said, "That's absolutely amazing. I have never seen anything like that." He replied, "Why does that amaze you brother Hall? Elijah did it." My friend Margie was not so sure and never saw this as anything but a coincidence. But Patsy and I were there and will always believe that at the request of a saintly old Haitian Christian God shut up the heavens "that it rained not" so the good news of Jesus could be preached in this strong voodoo area and his church be established. The church of Christ at Neil would go on to become a strong witness in this dark part of the island.

    On another night Hollins and I had gone to a small village called "Hatte Grammont" to preach. We always jokingly called it "Hot Grandma." We turned off the main road and drove through fields and paths to reach the spot we were to preach that night. As I drove very slowly through crowds of people at the edge of the village a huge man dressed only in a cut off pair of shorts and ragged shirt suddenly appeared directly in front of the truck. He raised both fists and brought them down hard, leaving dents in the hood of our truck. As I sat in shock, Hollins leaped from the truck, grabbed the man by his shirt, and said, "Buddy, if you touch our truck once more I'm going to deck you!" The bully pulled away and disappeared into the darkness and the huge crowd erupted with cheers. Hollins went on to preach that night from the back of our truck.

For a long period while we served in Haiti the church in Museville, VA supplied us with Bibles in the French language to distribute to the people. Cathy Hayes, wife of the minister Steve Hayes, did an outstanding job heading this up. She would order these by the case and we would carry them into the country. The custom officials never objected to us bringing them in. They knew the more Bibles, the better the citizens. Bible distribution has always been a part of our mission work. We are currently doing this in Africa even as I write. We would give them out at seminars and put them in sacks on the backs of mules to be carried over the high mountains where Bibles were scarce. Only eternity will reveal the good that was done by the Bibles distributed across this hurting land.

Earlier in the book I promised to say more about the Tonton Macutes (Bogeymen) used by the Duvaliers throughout Haiti. Two years after Papa Doc was elected President he began having trouble with the army, so he organized a group called Volunteers for National Security. In reality they were his own private army or secret police. They would become known as Tonton Macutes or Bogeymen. This was a reference to the mythological tale that a bogeyman would come get little children who were unruly and put them in a gunnysack (macute) and take them away where they would be eaten for breakfast. The Haitians called the Tontons "Uncle Gunnysack." By the time the last Duvalier was ousted from office there would be 300,000 Tonton Macutes spread all across Haiti. They ruled by intimidation and terror and were supposed to be the eyes of the President. Tontons wore blue denim shirts and dark sunglasses. There were always two in our town who just sat and watched what was going on both day and night. Armed with a pistol and machete, it is reported they killed more than 100,000 people during the Duvalier reign. They would tie their victims bodies in trees or anyplace they could be seen. This would serve as a warning to others. They would not engage in conversation with anyone and reported any thing they saw or heard to the President. The Duvalier dynasty lasted for 29 years and the Tonton Macutes were credited with keeping them in power. They were not paid a salary but made their living by theft and extortion. Needless to say they were hated by the people. Every one of them I knew practiced voodoo. I did not know a single one of them to ever become a Christian. They believed Duvalier was Jesus Christ incarnate and referred to him as "Voodoo Jesus."

As we began to develop the land we saw the need for a school. The children in Dessalines were forced to walk for miles if they went to school. They would leave before daybreak and return home when it was almost dark. We began with K through grade 3 and added a new grade each year until we reached grade 9. The parents paid a small amount for their children to attend and this was divided among the teachers. We raised some support to help with teachers' salary and supplies. The school was a good thing and caused us to be looked upon with appreciation from the community. We could teach whatever we liked as long as we taught Haitian history, math, and French. Of course the Bible was our main text book and all teachers were Christians. It was necessary to turn children away when we reached an enrollment of 300 students. We simply could not handle more than that. Each child was fed lunch each day, usually consisting of rice and beans. The organization CARE gave us thousands of pounds of rice and beans with no obligation on our part except a promise not to sell it. This was often the only meal some of our children would receive throughout the week. It was quite common to see these one hundred pound sacks of grain for sale in the market even though they were marked, "Gift of the American people - Not for sale." We knew the crooked Duvalier government was ripping off our beloved homeland, but there was nothing we could do about it. In

1986 when Baby Doc Duvalier was overthrown there was much violence and looting throughout the land and most of the warehouses owned by CARE were looted and torched. CARE pulled their workers and trucks out of Haiti and to my knowledge have never returned. The school continued to educate the children and a great number went on to attend high school at Goniaves.

About the same time the school was started we opened a small free medical clinic on the property. Patsy contacted doctors in North Carolina and was given great amounts of medicine and supplies. Doctors are given sample medicine that often expires and is thrown away. She collected this and bought as much as we were able. The main maladies seemed to be scabies, worms, colds, ear aches, open sores, and the like. She came upon a book entitled, "Where There Is No Doctor." It contained a wealth of information about tropical diseases and how to treat them. She found one of the best (and cheapest) treatments for lice and scabies was to mix sulphur with Vaseline and apply it to the patient. We carried Pediolyte in for the babies as well as vitamins and cough syrup. Quite often I would awaken before daylight and look out our window toward the clinic. My heart would break as I saw a great crowd of women holding their babies as they waited for Patsy to open it. She often would run out of medicine and have to close down until more could be collected. After a couple of years, Rosemary Almy from Missouri and Pat Snyder from Illinois joined us to work in the clinic. Both of these Christian ladies were widows and in excellent health. Both had medical backgrounds and did an outstanding job directing this part of the work. Patsy worked well with them and was thankful to have them on board. On occasions we would have American doctors or dentists come for short periods to assist.

Safe water was always a problem in the early days. Patsy would boil our water, but this took valuable fuel oil which was expensive even in the 1970s. We found a nice spring in the mountain about 700 yards above the development and piped it down to the property. We installed a holding tank but still didn't trust the water to be safe to drink. I had been told there were no well drillers in all of Haiti and had just about given up finding one when one day on my way to town I saw an old rig out in the field. It was the punch type like Patsy's dad had used for years. I stopped the truck and walked out to the rig which was running full tilt. The man operating it was middle aged and white with a full beard. When he introduced himself as Mr. Miller, I knew he was Amish and learned he was from Indiana. His only ministry in Haiti was drilling water wells. That's why he had come here and he had drilled a number of wells. I told him where we were and what we were trying to accomplish and asked if there would be any chance he could drill us a well. He explained that he had two more to drill and would be happy to bring his rig to Dessalines and sink us a well. The only cost would be for the fuel and the casing. It was almost two months later that he came and drilled a well on the property. It was deep and the water was cool. We put a hand pump on it and for the first time we had good, safe water. We had fenced the ten acres in order to keep animals out and before Mr. Miller had moved his rig we realized the people would destroy our fence coming in for water. We then asked him if he would drill another just on the edge of the road and off of our property. He was glad to do this and now the people in town had their own well with plenty of water. It is always the women's job to carry the water and how happy they were not to have to walk a mile or more for this.

I've always enjoyed sharing a joke or funny story, and Hollins and I shared the same ones with each other over and over for sixteen years. I described him earlier as a tall, handsome man with a great smile and glowing personality. He was in his late 60s when we began working together. He was always dressed in blue jeans, a cowboy hat, and western boots. One day we made the long trip to Port au Prince to purchase lumber and building supplies. Before returning home we decided to have lunch and went to a place called Round Pointe. After we were seated I noticed a woman staring at us and whispering to another woman with her. Finally she got up and came to our table and with much delight she said to Hollins, "I know you! I'm so surprised to see you in Haiti. I've seen all your movies. You're John Wayne." At that Hollins stood and touched the brim of his hat, and in his best western drawl he said, "Howdy, Ma'm." We laughed halfway back to Dessalines. When I asked him why he didn't tell her she was mistaken, he said, "Brother Hall, somewhere in this city of millions there is a lady telling all her women friends that she shook the hand of the Duke. What harm will it do to let her have her moment?"

Once Hollins eneterd a drug store as a little French lady was leaving. Unknown to Hollins her husband's name was Dedo. She had come to get some medicine for him, and as Hollins met her he tipped his hat and said, "How de do?" She exclaimed, "Oh! you know Dedo? He's been very sick. I'll tell him you asked about him." He always laughed deeply when he told this.

Having been raised in the Catholic church and being groomed to be a priest himself, Hollins loved to tell funny stories about these. He said the depot manager called the priest one day and said, "Father Calahan, you need to come pick up your books. They came in on the last train and they are leaking."

He said the Circus came to town when he was a boy and some of the workers had come to confess. The priest asked if they would do some of their tumbling tricks since he wouldn't have time to attend their performance. They were in the midst of doing these when two little Cajun ladies came to confess. One of them said to the other, "Oh dear. The Father is in a bad mood. I hope he doesn't make me do that for penance. The elastic is worn out in my bloomers."

We were having afternoon coffee one day when old Rappado knocked at our door. He was holding his head and said, "Oh Amigo, would you please give me a chapeau? (hat) The sun is so hot." Hollins asked, "Rappado, what size chapeau do you wear?" He replied, "Size thirty two." Hollins assured him he didn't have a hat that large but asked, "How do you know you wear a thirty two?" Rappado scratched his brown head and said, "Well, the shirt you gave me is sixteen and my head is twice the size of my neck." But my size 7 - 1/8 just fit so he went away happy.

During the eighties thousands of Haitians launched from the shores around Goniaves trying to make it to America. Great numbers of them died at sea, while others were turned back by the U.S. Coast Guard and brought back to Haiti where they suffered at the hands of the authorities. A few did make it to America. We could never understand why the Cubans were welcomed but the Haitians turned back. What the Haitians were trying to escape was every bit as bad as communism. One young man from Goniaves asked us for a job laying block on our church building. He was a good worker and worked about ten days and then didn't show up anymore. His friends were quite vague regarding his whereabouts but someone finally told us he had gone to America. More than a month later he came and asked for his job back. As we ate our lunch that day he told the most amazing story. Some man in Goniaves had an old rickety sailboat. It had no motor or navigational equipment and only a homemade sail. He was looking for ten people wishing to go to America. They would pay him $100 each and he would get them in sight of the Florida coast where they would all abandon the boat and make it anyway they could to shore. They all knew it was a big gamble but he believed it was worth trying, even if he died at sea. He told us how he had spent 18 days on the high seas in this overcrowded boat. It leaked badly and they were constantly bailing it out. They were being scorched by the sun by day and drenched by blowing rain at night. There was no room to lay down for sleep and bathroom facilities was a bucket they passed around. After a week all water and food was gone and by the second week the first of the passengers died and was dropped overboard. After 14 days and nights all but three of the eleven were dead and buried at sea. They drifted into St. Martien on the 18th day where the three received some medical treatment and food and were promptly returned to Haiti. I remember asking him if he would try that again. He smiled and replied, "As soon as I save another $100 and find a boat going."

After some time the preaching of the Gospel began to irritate some in town in spite of the other good things we were doing, and so it should not have been too great a surprise when two policemen showed up at our job site one morning with papers summoning us to court. I knew it was serious but couldn't understand their Creole and asked Hollins what it was about. He said "We are accused of making derogatory statements against the country. Have you made any remarks to anyone?" I assured him I had not and he then asked, "Did you say to John, 'what good is freedom if everyone is starving?'" I then remembered saying that. He had taken it completely out of context and reported it to the authorities. I immediately took Patsy to the airport to return home until this was resolved. I had no idea how this would go. The day of our court appearance the man who had reported me and made similar charges against Hollins had a hard time looking at us in court. We had been good to him and even treated his children in the clinic. Two of his children were students in our school. Hollins stared him down in the courtroom and when their eyes met Hollins mouthed, "Get him, devil." Court hearings are different in Haiti than in America. We had no one to defend us and proceedings began by several charges being made against us. We were not allowed to speak until all charges had been read and all witnesses had testified against us. Several people came in off the street and spoke against us and left. We had never met them. Finally we were allowed to answer the charges and Hollins elected to speak in our behalf. He told why we had come to Dessalines and what we had been doing in the past few years. He then said to the young judge, "Your honor, if we were not interested in helping this country we would still be in America. Our work and daily lives will speak for us. We are not guilty of any of these charges brought against us today." With that short speech he sat down. The judge said, "We'll take a short break and I'll give you my ruling." He then left the room for his chambers. In a short time he returned and announced that all charges against us were dismissed. Turning to John he said, "If you bother these men again or hinder their work in any way I will see to it that you go to prison." With that he dismissed the court.

    I went to the airport one morning to check on a flight home. I parked in the airport parking lot, checked with the airlines, and returned to the truck. As I drove out onto the main highway a policeman who was standing by the road motioned for me to stop.

Pointing to the sticker on the windshield he informed me it had expired and I couldn't drive it until I had the new one. I told him I would drive directly to the police station and get it. He proceeded to tell me I couldn't do that but that he would drive me there and I could buy the sticker and be on my way. I was suspicious but allowed him to drive as we went to the station about two miles away. When he pulled into the police compound he stopped the truck, took the keys and said, "Get out of the truck. It now belongs to the Grenada Police Force." When I protested loudly and asked how he could confiscate my truck he replied that I had abandoned it at the airport and they were allowed to take any abandoned vehicles. He then informed me that if I didn't leave the compound I would be arrested and locked up. I had no choice but to leave. As I walked down the street wondering what to do next I saw the American flag flying from a walled compound. I walked closer and saw that it was the U.S. Embassy. There were several U.S. Marines standing guard at the entrance. After showing my passport and being allowed to enter I was given a cold Coke and an American newspaper while I waited for someone to come and discuss my problem. I was wearing a baseball cap with the word "Virginia" across the front. Soon a man in a business suit came bounding down the steps. When he saw me he called out, "Virginia!" He asked where I was from and told me his home was near Culpepper. After telling him what had happened with the truck, he excused himself and went back upstairs. After a short time he returned and said if I would go back to the police compound my truck would be ready. When I got back the truck was sitting there with the new sticker on it and the keys inside. I got in it and drove home. Sure made me appreciate that Culpepper boy.

   It was quite rewarding to preach and teach in Haiti. It was a rich mission field, and the people were hungry to hear the truth and eager to obey it. Shortly after we began working there my brother-in-law, Jack Aaron printed several thousand baptismal certificates for our use. These were gone in a few years. Hollins estimated that in all the areas we worked we had about 11,000 baptisms. More than thirty churches were established throughout the Artibonite

Valley and beyond Hinche near Circa Cavejal on the Dominican border. Only a few of these had permanent buildings in which to meet but in all of them the Lord's supper was spread each Lord's day and the Bible was preached. It has been my dream to return and visit as many of these churches as possible before my earthly journey ends. Patsy remembers the beautiful evenings when the church would walk to the town spring, singing as we walked, and witness souls being obedient to Christ in baptism. These were happy days when we had boundless energy, good health, and great vision to do God's work. We had the support and prayers of family and friends and it was such joy to be serving in this poor but needy country.

A very young Mother brought a newborn baby to the clinic one day and placed her in Patsy's arms. Her name was Bonita, and she was only days old. Patsy tried to give her formula from a baby bottle but she was so weak she had no suck reflexes. So she put formula in a medicine dropper and fed her like a bird, just a few drops at a time. The other nurses and Patsy sent the mother home and told her they would do what they could for little Bonita, and when she was strong they would send for her. Bonita lived with us and the other two nurses for about seven months. When she was strong enough to return home she was trying to walk in a walker we had brought in. Bonita would be about 31 years old today. She was a happy and pleasant baby and brought us much joy. What a wonderful thought that we might greet her again in Heaven. I sure pray that we will.

Once while we were busy about the work at Dessalines someone came for Patsy. She learned that a small boy had fallen into an open fire and was badly burned. He had severe burns about his face and neck and she knew she would be unable to treat him as needed. His family placed him in back of our Daihatsu truck, and with two men going along in the event blood donors were needed, Patsy began the long drive to the famous Albert Schweitzer Hospital. It was about four hours away and over dirt roads filled with huge potholes. It was a dangerous and exhausting trip but they finally arrived at the hospital. Patsy had bandaged his face in order to keep the dust from his burns and only one eye was visible. He never made a sound. They carefully carried him inside only to be told that they couldn't accept him. Patsy pleaded to know why and they said he had never been there before and they had no file on him. She continued to plead with them saying, "I can't carry him back home. If I do he will die." Finally out of sheer exhaustion and desperation she sat down in the middle of the floor and began to cry. They then found a mattress, laid him on it, and admitted him. This sweet child died through the night, but not until my caring wife had done all she could to save him.

Patsy could write her own book about treating sick and dying people in Haiti. Having a medical clinic in a place like Haiti is like owning a dairy operation. You can't just walk away whenever you desire. People would come everyday but Sunday for medicine or treatment and often some would come to our house or the church building even on Sunday. In 1984 our good friend, Dr. Ross Nash of Charlotte, NC came to do dental work in our small clinic. Keep in mind that we had no electricity except a small generator. He brought some small instruments with him and on Monday he began extracting teeth from a long line of people who had been hurting too long. Patsy was assisting Dr. Nash and after about an hour she came to the house saying she just couldn't help him anymore. The heat and the sight of so much blood had made her sick. I assured her that I certainly couldn't assist him and there was no one else to help. We held hands and prayed and asked God to help her finish the job. She washed her face and returned to the clinic where she assisted him for the entire two weeks he was with us.

There were things that made us laugh every day in and around Dessalines. One of our finest preachers was Ernie Etinene. Hollins had baptized him and we trained him to preach. He was also an excellent carpenter so it was with that trade he made his living. Séance was an older man in the church and when he became sick he called for Hollins to come pray with him before he died. His wife, being much younger, came to Ernie to order a casket for her husband. Ernie crafted it from pine boards and lined it with burlap. Since he had no place to store it he brought it to Séance's house. When his wife brought it into their small house Séance saw it and suddenly began feeling better. In a short time he was up and about and demanding the casket be removed from his house. It was stored in one of our sheds until the family needed it, and it was not Séance but his wife who was buried in it.

No one knew how old Rappado was. His name means "brown sugar." He was probably in his 70s when we first met him. He had no relatives as far as anyone knew. He lived in a small shack in town and ate wherever he could find someone who would feed him. He didn't come to our door every day but almost every day, and Patsy nor Hollins either one ever turned him away. Even if it was only a piece of bread they would give him something. He told this amazing story with such consistency that we believed him. He declared that when he was a young boy living near Cap Haitien a band of men kidnaped him as he returned about dark from working in a rice field. They walked many days until they crossed the border into the Dominican Republic. There they sold him as a slave to a large plantation owner. He worked in his fields for years from sunrise until sundown. He learned to speak Spanish from those he worked with. He always called me Amigo. He would often greet me saying, "Hey Amigo, give me ten cents." One day after he was a grown man he just walked away from his bondage and headed in the direction of Haiti. When he stumbled into Dessalines he decided to stay and had been there ever since. Diabetes caused him to go blind toward our last days there and Séance became his constant companion, leading him along by having him hold to a stick while he held the other end. He was buried in one of Ernie's fine crafted caskets and awaits the resurrection of the dead where there are no slaves, diabetics, or homeless persons. When the saints go marching in I fully expect to hear him say, "Hey Amigo!"

We could have never built the buildings for new congregations without the teams that came down for a week or two at a time. I wish we had kept a record but we know they numbered in the hundreds. We had teams that came every other year or so from Virginia, North Carolina, Kentucky, Indiana, Louisiana, Texas, Florida, and Ohio. These were men who had building skills and could do jobs in which I had little ability. They brought their own tools and often brought their wives who would help with cooking each day. These men worked hard in the hot sun all day as they tried to accomplish as much as they could while there. One morning a young Haitian girl about twenty stopped at the house and asked if she could prepare the noon meal while the men were working. We knew her and assumed she was a good cook or wouldn't have asked for the job. The men came in at noon, washed up, and sat down at our large table anxious to see what Haitian dish she had prepared. Someone gave thanks and removed the cloth she had placed over the meal to keep the flies away. There on the table was a huge bowl of popcorn.

I've always been bad about bringing someone home to eat with us without telling Patsy about it beforehand. One day I asked brother Leon Decade home for dinner. When we went in the house Patsy looked alarmed and called me aside. She whispered that we had no food for her to prepare. Holding a box in her hand she whispered, "All we have is this box of instant potato pancakes." I went back where brother Decade was sitting and said, "My brother, would you like potato pancakes for your dinner?" He thought a moment and said, "Brother Hall, I would like potato pancakes for *part* of my dinner."

For the first year Patsy and I shared a house with Hollins so we ate every meal together. She would cook on a two burner kerosene stove and could put some good meals on the table from it. We usually ate around 5:00PM so we would have time to get to church services that might be going on at seven. There was a young man in the church who began showing up at supper time each night. Not wishing to appear rude, one of us would say, "Noe, would you like to stay for dinner?" He always said yes. He was not a poor man and neither was he hungry. I guessed he liked Patsy's cooking and American food so that's why he came. This went on for a long time and one night when he came, Hollins was swatting flies and saving them on a paper plate. He said to Noah, "You'll love dinner tonight. When I get enough we're going to make fly soup." With raised eyebrows Noe asked, "Do you eat flies?" Hollins replied, "Well, if the flies can eat my food, I should be able to eat them." Suddenly Noe remembered he had to see a man in town about something and wouldn't be able to stay for dinner. He excused himself and left.

There were no paved roads where we lived so our truck was always covered with a heavy coat of dust. We began noticing when we got up each morning that the truck had been cleaned inside and out. We had no clue who was doing this and no one seemed to know. This went on for several weeks and we could never determine how this was happening. Finally I noticed an old blanket in our tool shed as if someone was sleeping there. I got up in the night and checked it out and there was a young boy about 15 years old. His name was Sargis and he had no family and nowhere to live. He began sleeping in our tool shed and paying for it by cleaning the truck in the night. We took him in and from then on he ate his meals at our table. We provided a cot for him to sleep on and he was a valuable and trusted worker. We paid him a modest salary for his work and we watched him grow into a strong man in his twenties. When he was 25 he applied for a passport and went to America legally. The last I heard he was married with two children and owned his own concrete finishing business in the Miami, FL area. I've always been glad he was able to escape the impossible life in Haiti for the better life in America.

I've already written about the great privilege and pleasure to work with a man like Hollins Duhon. He was truly a giant in the faith and I learned more from him than I could ever write in a book. But when you work with someone day in and day out there are bound to be differences. We didn't have many but I do recall a time when we sharply disagreed on a matter and things had been cool between us for a few days. We were having an evening service and after the song service our preacher Ernie brought a message on forgiveness. He very well could have known that we were in a dispute. I never asked him. But before the conclusion of the service they did something I have never before or since seen done in a Christian church. They brought out pans of water and without saying a word they began to wash each others feet. I had mixed emotions about this probably because I had not humbled myself to forgive or seek forgiveness. Suddenly Hollins kneeled before me, slipped off my shoes and began to wash my feet. I, in turn washed his feet. There in the building we embraced each other and cried tears of repentance and forgiveness. It's hard to feel anger toward someone who is washing your feet. I've been in a few churches where they need to break out the basins.

Nicodem was a small physically handicapped boy who never missed a gathering at church. He had a difficult time walking and would always sit by me when we gathered to worship. One night while sitting beside me he ran his small fingers over my watch. Then he touched my ring and picked up my flashlight. My camera was on the bench between us and he picked it up and studied it. With those big brown eyes looking into mine he whispered, "The American man has his hand on so many nice things." And so we do.

We never had air conditioning the entire time we lived in Haiti. The house had a tin roof with no insulation so it would heat up during the day and radiate at night. Since we didn't have electricity we couldn't use a fan either. Patsy and I always slept with the window open, but being at the base of a huge mountain we seldom got a breeze. After a long, hot day we had gone to bed when just outside our window a small dog began to bark. His owner had tied him with a rope. He went on and on with his irritating bark so that neither of us could sleep. Hollins' room was just down the hall from us and soon he was tapping at our door. I said, "Yes, brother Duhon?" He said, "Brother Hall, do you have your knife?" I replied that I did and he asked, "May I borrow it? I have to do something about the dog." I gave him my knife and heard the front door open as he went out. Soon we heard the dog yelping like he was dying and then he got quiet. Hollins came back, tapped on the door again and said, "Brother Hall, here is your knife." I exclaimed, "Did you kill the neighbor's dog?" He said, "No brother Hall. I cut his rope."

A tiny little grandma knocked at our door one day and asked to speak to Friar Duhon. When he came to see what she wanted, she said, "My dog was sleeping in the road and you passed over him with the truck." He said, "Oh grandma, I'm so sorry. I didn't see your dog. Is he hurt?" She said, "Friar Duhon, my dog is dead, and he was a hundred dollar dog." He told her he would find her another dog and asked what color she wanted. He said, "Do you want a blue or red or maybe a green dog?" She said, "Not a green one." He then said, "What if I just give you five dollars?" She said, "Oh, that would be fine."

Frederick worked around Dessalines Christian Development doing odd jobs. We mixed all cement by hand and he was usually in charge of this project. Every year his wife would leave him and go across the mountain. She would stay gone six or seven months and when she returned she would be pregnant. After the baby was born she would live with Frederick a few months and leave again. Then when she returned she would again be pregnant. Frederick always took her back and worked hard to raise the babies she had by someone else. Once when she sent word she was coming home for good a nice crowd from the church was at the bus stop when she arrived. We could see the bus stop from our house and I remarked to Patsy how nice it was that our people were so forgiving and willing to welcome her home. Then as I got a closer look I saw Frederick's wife standing all alone and the church folk had gathered around a 200 pound registered Yorkshire hog that someone had ordered.

Hollins and I drove to Port au Prince one morning to buy supplies. It was a long trip but that was about the only place you could find the things you really needed. We parked the truck near the Iron Market and were checking out some of the shops for whatever items we needed. I have never worn sunglasses and still don't, but the sun was so bright that I bought a cheap pair in one of the shops. As soon as we walked back onto the sidewalk I put them on and continued up the street. It helped with the glare but I was thinking I wouldn't be able to wear them because they were so dark I could barely see. When Hollins stepped off the sidewalk to cross the street, I followed him and suddenly stepped into an open sewer and sank to my chest in raw sewage. I scrambled out about as fast as I had fallen in, and there in a city of two million people I took off every stitch of clothing I had on. I took my wallet and passport out of my jeans and left jeans, shirt, underwear, socks, shoes, and sunglasses on the sidewalk. Wearing only my Cincinnati Reds baseball cap, I walked buck naked down the street until I came to a clothing store. I went inside and went directly to the men's room where I bathed in the sink. In a short while Hollins came in, saying he had lost me. I asked him, "Brother, how could you lose a naked white man wearing a red baseball cap in a city of two million black people?" He was biting his lip to keep from laughing. I waited in the bathroom while he picked out some new clothes for me. When I walked back out on the street I got almost as many stares as when I went in. I was wearing yellow pants, a purple and yellow shirt and purple socks. And of course I was wearing my red Cincinnati Reds cap but no sunglasses.

The entire time we worked in Haiti I was constantly having minor health issues. I refused to take the anti-malaria medicine because I had read it was hard on the liver. I had two minor cases of malaria but was over it in a few days so I wasn't greatly alarmed when I woke up one morning in 1984 feeling sick. Hollins had returned to Louisiana for a short stay and Patsy had gone home to get ready for Christmas, so I was alone there at Dessalines. I rested that day but in the evening began having chills and a high fever. It was much worse the next day so I packed my bags and headed for the airport. It was a difficult drive as sick as I was but I managed to make it. There were no flights going so I got a room at the Magic Bud, left the truck there for Hollins to pick up when he arrived, and flew out the next morning for the U.S. When I reached Miami I learned there was nothing going to Raleigh or Greensboro until the next morning. I would have to spend the night in Miami but I had a grand total of six dollars and some change and no credit card. I spent a really tough night at the airport with no place except the floor to lay down. It was cold from the A/C and my chills made it seem doubly so. One minute I would be freezing and the next minute I would be burning up. Malaria causes vomiting and I had been unable to eat anything for several days. During the night I would hallucinate and think I was at home talking with family members. I finally reached home and began to feel better. Even though Patsy insisted, I refused to see the doctor, thinking then it must have been a virus and I was on the mend. But in about 24 hours it hit me again and this time it was worse. Dr Council was a flying buddy and a good friend. He had been a M.A.S.H. doctor in Korea and had seen plenty of malaria. After looking at the blood work he sent me immediately to N.C. Baptist Hospital in Winston Salem. There my malaria was diagnosed as *falsipian* which was the worst type, but if I could survive it there would be no recurrences. They worked hard to get me stable but the malaria was destroying the platelets in my blood. With my rare blood type they had no platelets to give me. That night a baby with my blood type died at the hospital and they gave me its platelets. In two days I was up and walking around and in a week I went home. I never knew this baby's name or who its parents were but it has often made me think of another who gave his blood that we all might live eternally. Oh! I hope this is what my life has been about!

By 1986 the country of Haiti had finally had enough of the 29 year rule of the Father and son Duvaliers and Jean Claude was ousted from the office of President. We began to feel the pressure in October 1985 when we would go to Goniaves for supplies. The streets were always filled with demonstrators, and every week someone would be killed by the police. Road blocks were common, and those doing this demanded money to allow you to pass. Hollins and I became foolhardy in that we would often jump out of the truck and confront those blocking the road, sometimes tearing out their roadblocks and passing through them. I carried a large piece of two by four for protection. Hollins named it, "Lou's Ugly Stick." Their favorite blockade was large rocks and car tires. Sometimes they would set the tires on fire. Things became so dangerous that we began to seriously consider coming out and trying to work in a more peaceful place. We talked about the small island of Grenada another 750 miles from us. It had undergone a

U.S. invasion in 1983, and since we had no work there and they spoke English it might be a place we could work without turmoil. Little did we know that God would lead us there but the work would already be established when we arrived eight years later.

President Reagan began to pressure Baby Doc to step down but refused to allow him asylum in America. Finally when France agreed to accept him a U.S. Air Force plane flew in on February 7, 1986 and whisked him off the island. He carried with him a reported six million dollars plus what he had stashed in Swiss banks. This was money he made through drug deals heading to the U.S. and the selling of body parts of Haitians to medical schools around the world. A large number died during this overthrow but things became peaceful again almost overnight. It would remain fairly peaceful for the next four years. God blessed the years from 1986-1990 with great victory, and great numbers of souls were baptized into Christ. New churches of Christ were being established and young preachers were trained to preach for them throughout the entire Artibonite Valley. There seemed to be more freedom to travel throughout Haiti, and the spirit of the people rose greatly. They had to believe that things would get better and they prayed that their next president would lift them from poverty and turn the country around. Alas, it didn't happen and hasn't happened even in 2012.

In the 1990 election Jean Betrand Aristide was elected President in the first Democratic election ever in Haiti. He was a Catholic priest, very popular with the people, and received 65% of the vote. Eight months later he was deposed by a coup led by Army General Cedras who had been trained by the United States Army. Evidence was strong that our own C.I.A. had backed this coup. When we heard rumblings of bad things about to happen we decided to get out of Haiti. We made our way into Port au Prince and ran right into the middle of the violence. The streets were full of people and in all the confusion Patsy and I became briefly separated. We were in the city trying to get a flight on Eastern Airlines the next day. The soldiers were firing automatic rifles into the air. The flights were full, and they refused to honor Haitian currency or our credit cards. The airlines wanted American cash only. We learned later that five thousand died during this coup. We arrived at the airport the next morning and there was only one seat left on the flight. Patsy said she wasn't going without me and I said, "Oh yes, you are. It will be easier to take care of me than both of us." I promised to grab the next flight I could. After she went aboard I started to leave the airport, not knowing where I could take refuge from the violence. It seemed the entire city was fighting. Then an attendant from Eastern's desk called out to me saying there was another seat available. Someone had failed to show up. I'll never forget the smile on Patsy's face when she saw me come aboard. The plane was filled with missionaries, tourists, and business people all fleeing the country. When we took off there was a strange silence on the plane and as the fully loaded 727 climbed and turned toward America you could see the city burning below. Chris Herget and his wife of Christianville Mission was seated in front of me. They were white with fright and did not speak for a long time. For several minutes we flew in silence, and suddenly the entire plane erupted with cheers. The date of our departure was Monday, September 30, 1991 at 11:15 AM. In a little more than two hours we would be on American soil. I have an entry in my diary for that date which reads, "Thanks be to God who gives us the victory through Christ Jesus, our Lord."

    I have returned to Haiti only once in the twenty one years since we left and again was caught in the violence and unable to make it to Dessalines. Patsy returned once to visit our granddaughter Tiffany Hall who was doing mission work near Christianville. Our dear friend Hollins died in 2002 at age 84 and is buried in his beloved Cajun country in Louisiana. Brother Leon Decade, that great man of faith and prayer, died from complications from diabetes in 1993 and is buried at Cape Haitian. Rappado and his friend Seance both died at an age known only to God and were buried in Ernie's pine boxes on the mountain overlooking the church at Dessalines. The church in Dessalines has remained strong and continues to serve our Lord without the presence of an American missionary. What a great journey this was. I'm so glad we were there. Regrets? A few. I wish I had worked harder, prayed more, loved more, reached more. I am so looking forward to seeing these dear friends again when we meet on that shore where there are no goodbyes.

Louis with Hollins Duhon in Dessalines, Haiti

Above: Hollins Duhon cooking in Dessalines, Haiti

Below: Patsy caring for baby Paula in Dessalines, Haiti

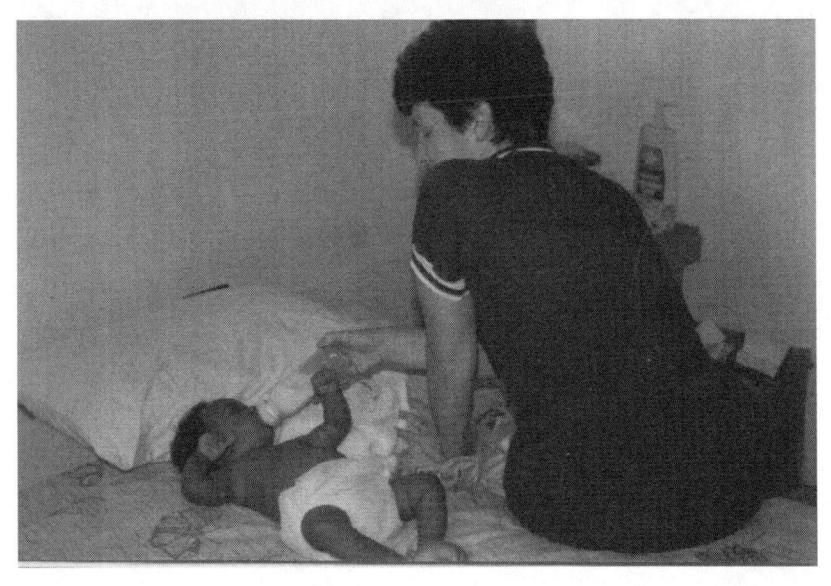

Above: Louis with Rappado in Dessalines, Haiti
Below: Ernie building a casket for Séance in Dessalines, Haiti

Above: Patsy's father Argel McBee in St. Marc, Haiti

## BACK IN AMERICA

I wasn't sure what I'd do next, but in June 1987 I'd preached a revival in Patrick County, VA in which 13 responded to the invitation, 10 of those by baptism. I loved the humble people of this church and community, and since that time I had served as part time preacher for them in between trips into Haiti. In the fall they asked me to come on a more regular basis and voted in favor of this. We could continue to live where we wanted and could also continue with my revival meetings. By 1988 we had slowly moved to the field as we became more and more involved in the work. As I had always done, I hit the road running in evangelism and began seeing many people come to Christ. One of the first I baptized was Sammy Mills, a humble man and friend to this day. I taught James Nester for four Thursday nights and baptized him on a stormy and rainy night. James went on to become an elder and one of the best Sunday school teachers I've ever heard. Junior and Ramona Cassady and one of their daughters obeyed the Gospel, and this fine couple brought their musical talents to be used of the Lord. They remain dear friends and a blessing to many. Almareane Gilley was a widow living in a shack in the hollow near the church. In a short time I baptized her. She remained faithful until her death. Ricky Burnette was baptized and we're Facebook friends even now. Many others came from other churches to work with Stella Christian. I performed many weddings and conducted numerous funerals of people I had come to love dearly.

By the spring of 1990 the present building was full and some began talking of building a new building. My friend Stuart Worthley from Kokomo, Indiana was called to come and talk with us. Stew was a very able church builder having constructed many in Indiana. He was hired to do the job and construction began immediately. I had mixed emotions about building. There was such a sweet spirit in this church and I wanted nothing to hinder that. When it was approved I did pledge to stay out of the discussion on what and how to build and to support it financially, and those I did. I constantly encouraged the people not to quit building the church while we're building a building. We never stopped visiting and teaching, and souls continued to obey the Lord. The building was built and the church moved in it in the fall because.... "The people had a mind to work."

By this time we had decided that we wanted to live here in these beautiful hills of Virginia so we bought six acres of land and made plans to build a house. Patsy and a friend of mine drew out the plan on a napkin as we sat at dinner one evening. In the meantime Patsy's Mom had a stroke in Ohio and we moved her to Virginia so Patsy could take care of her. She lived a year with us and returned home because she needed more treatment than we were able to give. She spent her last years at Sunny Slope nursing home in Ohio and died at age 84 in 1993. I have said many times that if every man had been blessed with a mother-in-law like I had there would have never been any mother-in-law jokes. I loved her dearly and she loved me. We never had the first disagreement. I preached her funeral. It was hard to say goodbye to this lovely lady. She had been baptized April 5, 1953 at Hopedale church of Christ.

In October and December of 1990 we drilled a well and put in a septic system on our land and in the early spring we began construction. It would take about a year to complete it enough to move in since we had agreed not to borrow money or finance it. By 1992 we were able to move into our new home where we have lived for the past twenty years. It's a comfortable place to live and we thank God for it daily, but we know at best it's temporary. We look forward to the one that's permanent in the heavens, whose builder and maker is God.

I enjoyed the ministry at Stella and worked with some wonderful people. They were unselfish with me and paid an excellent salary. They allowed me time to speak for revivals and men's retreats. But in 1993 I began to see a move taking place that I feared was designed to oust the elders. I told them this in one of our meetings but they couldn't see it. These were good men who dearly loved our Lord and his church. Perhaps they thought if they ignored it, it would go away on its own. I never knew since I've never discussed this with them since that time. I believed then and do today that elders are required to make those hard decisions that no one enjoys making. Nothing was addressed that week so on the Lord's day morning I resigned. I praised the elders for working with and supporting me. I made it clear that this decision was entirely mine and no one was forcing me out or asking me to leave. These statements were absolutely true. I left the church and not many months later the very thing I had predicted came to pass. In a congregational vote the elders were all dismissed. The day I heard it I sat down and cried. To my knowledge I have no enemies among this fine church. When we meet we smile and embrace. They choose to support our mission work and have for a long time. We continue living about two miles from the church building because we love them and they remain our friends. I have preached for them since and I am scheduled to preach for them again a few days from now. Two of the elders were asked to serve again sometime later and both are doing so today.

  I was 58 years old and convinced we had time to work on another mission field, but where? My revival schedule was filling for the coming year and there would be plenty I could do here. We even talked of establishing a new church somewhere. There were a number of churches looking for ministers and two of them had contacted us. One of them in Indiana was in a great position to grow and appeared challenging but I had really missed foreign work and was praying that God might open a door somewhere.

  One night my friend Tim Stamper of Kentucky called me and asked if I would be interested in going to Grenada on a mission trip with him. He explained that he had friends from Kentucky Christian College by the name of Jim and Becky Newman who had been working in Grenada, West Indies since about 1986. Jim had invited him down and Tim thought I might also be interested. Tim had become a good friend after I held him a revival and he had even visited us in Haiti a number of times. My heart jumped at this. Hollins and I had discussed going to Grenada in 1985 but never had. Tim's wife, Sandi and his daughter, Andrea would go also. This would be a two week trip and would give us opportunity to see the work the Newmans were doing and decide if this would be a place we could serve. Jim and Becky were working alone, having had several Americans work with them and return to the states.

Patsy and I agreed to go with the Stampers on this trip and the five of us flew out of Raleigh-Durham on November 18, 1993. American Airlines was having labor problems and talk of a strike by their workers had been in the news for several days. We were assured by the airlines that we would not be stranded, so when Fox 23 news channel stuck the camera in my face and asked, "Are you concerned about the current situation with American Airlines?" I answered, "No." We left Miami early the next morning, walking through striking AA workers to get to our plane. From Miami we flew to San Juan only to learn that out flight to Grenada had been canceled because of the strike. Through small commuter planes we island hopped to St. Lucia and then to Barbados and finally into Grenada. We had spent a night in Miami and a night in St. Lucia, but at last we were on the Spice Island of Grenada in the West Indies. When I stepped off the plane into the warm sunshine and sweet aroma of spices I had the feeling this could be the place I would work for the rest of my life.

We spent two weeks meeting the church people and exploring the island. Tim and I both spoke several times each. I was taken by the beauty of this tropical island. Its white sand and blue waters along with the lush green forests and the smiles of the brown skinned people with British accents was quite a contrast to what we had experienced in Haiti. Though there was poverty I saw no starving or dying people. We had lived sixteen years with violence and political unrest and there was none of that here. It's true we had come from a nation of six and one half million to one of one hundred thousand, but the Gospel needed to be preached here as well. Patsy and I loved Jim and Becky Newman immediately. Jim was as conservative as Hollins Duhon had been except he was more the scholar and an excellent teacher. His home church was Lawshe church at Seaman, Ohio. I had preached revival there in 1962. Jim laughed and said he was in the nursery that week. I think it's fair to say that Jim had a dry wit about him that would sometimes take me by surprise. Becky was from Hillsboro, Ohio. She and Jim had met while in bible college. We love Becky so much that it's hard for me to describe what she was like. Friendly and very accommodating, everyone at Jean Anglias church loved her dearly. She taught several of the adults to read and taught children Bible stories that have made a difference in their lives twenty years later. Becky is blessed with a beautiful singing voice and used it to the glory of God. They had two small boys, Daniel and Andrew who are now adults and serve with them in Australia. Jim was the only person I had ever met who loved pinto beans as much as I did and it didn't hurt any that he was an avid Cincinnati Reds baseball fan. At the end of the two weeks I asked them if they wanted help and they both answered "yes." Patsy and I were confident God had opened another door and we were anxious to enter.

Our house in Patrick Springs, VA

## GRENADA, WEST INDIES

We spent a happy December in Virginia, getting ready for Christmas and telling friends about our decision to work in Grenada. My 1993 diary records my preaching at area churches in Virginia and North Carolina and looking forward to returning to Grenada in January.

Unfortunately my diaries for 1994 and 1995 are missing so I must write from memory of these two years. Some of the events in revival are recorded earlier in the book. We were working with only the one church that Jim had established in 1986. It was a congregation of around eighty with a large number of small children. Many of these children rode our buses to church and came from non-Christian homes. They had never been taught and were often noisy and unruly during services. I found that hard to deal with coming from Haiti where discipline was strict. Though the church has matured greatly in twenty years, even today no one thinks anything of getting up and walking outside or going back to the restroom in the middle of the message. Once while I was teaching, about five or six adults jumped up and ran outside. This was in the old building and I could see them all standing in the yard looking up at the sky. After a few minutes they came back and took their seats. Before I continued speaking, I asked, "Maria, did you see the Concorde?" She replied, "No, brother Hall. It's too cloudy."

We enjoyed the change of pace in Grenada. Unlike in Haiti, almost everyone in Grenada had a job and so they were busy during the day. This gave us time to study and prepare sermons and lessons as well as relax and rest for any evening activities at church. The Lord's day was full with Sunday school and worship in the morning and evening. In addition to that, Jim and I drove the two buses to bring people to church which took two hours or more every Sunday. We conducted Bible study on Thursday night and again drove the buses an hour before and an hour after the services. Usually a couple of nights each week were set aside to teach the men who aspired to teach and preach. They had many hours of preparation from both Jim and myself. Patsy and Becky stayed busy teaching the women and children. Vacation Bible School was conducted each July with a team coming from America to lead this. A couple of revivals or crusades were conducted sometime through the year.

In these early years we saw the attendance rise and fall in the church. Sometimes the attendance would reach seventy five or eighty and then suddenly it would drop to forty. I really tried to understand the problem and finally concluded that it was several things. First, the church was established with young and immature people who had no church background or depth to their faith. They would be coming and working hard when some small matter would side track them and turn them from the church. It didn't have to be much. A word spoken the wrong way could do it and often did. Secondly, being young and lacking spiritual roots, immorality would creep in and bring havoc on the members. I can think of several of our young unmarried girls who were active in the church and became pregnant and we saw them no more. Sometimes they would come back after the baby was born and repent of that sin, only to go out and repeat it all over again. It was a constant battle as we took three steps forward and two steps back. Twenty years down the road this situation would improve greatly.

Working with Jim and Becky was truly a pleasure. Jim was younger than our son but never treated me like an old man. We worked together day after day without a cross word or disagreement. We shared in the preaching and teaching and sometimes would conduct a special series from one of the books in the Bible or a topical study. The food and the weather in Grenada always agreed with me. The stomach problems I had constantly battled in Haiti never happened anymore and my health was excellent. I continued to conduct many revivals between trips in and out of Grenada and God was blessing the preaching of his word as he always had.

Patsy and I had both been studying for our Amateur Radio license and in December 1995 received these from the government of Grenada. Her callsign was J37LG and mine was J37LH. Prior to this we had received our General class licenses back home in Virginia. We did not yet have a radio in Grenada but Jim did and freely offered us use of it. It was a great joy to talk with our son, Doug back in North Carolina. We would eventually set up our own station and used it daily until the Internet and e-mail became available on the island. One Christmas morning when feeling a little blue, we kept our schedule with Doug in America and as we talked we could hear the happy shouts and laughter of our grandchildren as they opened their presents. We both cried a little. Doug would patch us in by phone to our other children, Tammy and Brenda so we enjoyed having contact with the family. Today we can call all over America from Grenada, anytime day or night for a mere twenty dollars per year. What a blessing.

In 1996 the crime rate in Grenada suddenly jumped. Two of the medical students from the University of Saint Georges were mugged while out jogging. Scotia Bank was robbed in broad daylight and a great number of home invasions took place. Jim and Becky's home was broken into while they were on a short visit to the states. Several items were taken and the house was throughly ransacked. The contents of their file cabinet were scattered about the room and food was thrown everywhere. At about the same time our house was entered when someone removed a window air conditioner and went inside. Nothing was disturbed, but several cameras and a few other items were taken. We must have surprised them in the act since we found the cameras and air conditoner in the grass in the back yard the next day. For the next two nights I sat in the darkness of our living room with a baseball bat (I had left my "Ugly Stick" in Haiti) waiting for someone to come and finish the job, but no one ever came back. When the weekly newspaper came out we read that a large number of prisoners had been released from the prison at Richmond Hill. Most people believed they were responsible since crime had been fairly low before that. It was a disturbing thing to know that someone had violated your privacy by illegally entering your home. I went to the police station to report it but they showed little concern and never came to check it out. I asked the policemen in charge what would happen to me if

I hurt someone breaking in. He replied, "Nothing, just be sure you do a complete job. We don't want to have to deal with them." I was glad it never came to that.

By the end of 1996 Jim and I realized the church would never become an indigenous church unless we eased out and turned more of the leadership and responsibility over to the local people. Jim had taught Roger Edwards and Rodney Thomas and baptized them both into Christ. We had both spent many hours teaching them the Bible and how to teach and preach. We had invited talented people from the states to come for leadership seminars. A Professor from one of our bible colleges had conducted classes for us. Jim Newman is extremely talented in writing Bible lessons and good solid material and had constantly provided these to them. They had Bibles and textbooks to assist in equipping them for ministry. These men could do it if we got out of the way and allowed them to. So in early December we asked them to meet with us on a Monday night. Tim Stamper was again visiting the island and the five of us met on the front porch of our house at Coral Cove. Roger and Rodney were stunned at the announcement we would be leaving. We shared with them our plans to come back often in the coming year and for as long as it took and continue to teach them as they gradually took over the responsibility of the church. Rodney spoke first and in essence said, "If you quit, we quit." I answered by saying they had been taught and had obeyed the Gospel. A year before we had ordained them as evangelists. They knew the truth and if they turned from it or quit, they would answer to God. I challenged them to see that this was a great opportunity and that God had been preparing them for this time. Rodney spoke again and said, "My wife and I will stay with the church if we are the only ones there." This fine man of God has been true to his word. Because of marital problems a few years later, Roger Edwards left the church but since that time other men have stepped up. Trevon Griffith is a deacon and helps in teaching and preaching. Deon Griffith attended Windward Island School Of Evangelism and is associate evangelist with Rodney and alternates in preaching and teaching. Rodney Thomas continues to serve as evangelist with Jean Anglais church of Christ. His wife Maria is ever by his side in God's work.

In October of 1997 I had returned to Grenada to teach. Patsy had remained at home because of the serious illness of her dad, Argel McBee in Ohio. She had gone to take care of him since he lived alone. After a teaching session on the night of the 18th I called her and she said, "Louis, I'm afraid Dad's not going to make it through the night." I so much wanted to be with Patsy at this time in her life. Her Mom was gone and now cancer was taking its toll on her Dad. Here I was several thousand miles from her on a small island and maybe days away from seeing her. I called a travel agent and was told I could get out the next morning if I didn't mind flying to Dallas, Texas and back to North Carolina. From North Carolina I would pick up my car and drive to Ohio. It wasn't likely I could get there before he died, but it was worth a try. I left Grenada airport at 6 AM and flew to San Juan. From San Juan I flew to Texas and then to Raleigh, NC. From Raleigh I drove through Virginia stopping at our house to shower, change clothes, and pick up my blue suit and tie, and continued the eight hour drive to Ohio. It was after 10 PM when I pulled into the old farm house. There was a small light on in the living room. I prayed I was in time and could be a comfort to my dear wife and her Dad. I rejoiced to find him still alive and sat down by his bed. I took his hand and told him I was here and everything was going to be fine. I then asked him to squeeze my hand if he could hear me. He squeezed it. After less than an hour, while I had my right hand on the back of his neck, he quietly relaxed and was gone. "Papaw" as my children and grandchildren all called him, had lived 84 years on this earth. He was one of the most unusual men I ever met. No one ever loved children any more than he did and they loved him as well. Even today when our family get's together, someone is always telling something funny he said or did. I preached his funeral two days later and have always been thankful that God allowed me to be with he and Patsy before he died.

Jim and I continued to make many trips into Grenada where we would stay weeks at a time. This time would be spent in intense study with the church and doing our best to train and equip an able and faithful leadership. In 2003 Jim and Becky would move to Australia where they are doing an outstanding job in reaching and training. They have returned to Grenada several times to assist in teaching and came back for the 25th anniversary of the church in 2011.

Patsy and I have continued to work with the church in Grenada, and this section of the book is being written while we are here in November and December 2011. In March we will return to conduct evangelistic services. It is our plan to work with this church until God calls us home. It's true they have grown and matured in many ways and are truly an indigenous church but we have become a part of each other. We know and feel their love like no other church we've ever served and we love them dearly. We will soon celebrate twenty years with them. Patsy informed me recently that if I went home before her she would continue to return to Grenada and serve where she could. That made me happy. I realized not long after we first came to Grenada that this work would never grow like the work in Haiti. Grenada is a resistant field. I'm not sure why. It could be because every denomination one can imagine has come here and false teaching is rampant. Maybe it's the Catholic influence leading the people to believe they are already OK and don't need the Gospel. I recently asked one of the men why it was so hard to reach people with the gospel here and he answered, "Indifference." Another reason is that though Grenada is not a rich country, neither is it poor like Haiti. Most of the people have little trouble providing for their families so see little need of God in their lives. However it's viewed by others, the work for Christ in Grenada can be clearly seen as a success story. There is a strong witness for new testament Christianity on this island that was not here prior to 1986.

On September 7, 2004 hurricane Ivan struck the island with devastating force. It killed 39 of its residents and injured scores more. More than 90% of houses and buildings suffered damage and great numbers were completely destroyed. Electric and phone lines were down for many days. Roads were destroyed and air transportation was shut down for one week. Then limited flights were allowed for the next few days. The nutmeg crops were destroyed and fruit trees were laid waste throughout the country. Our church buildings were either destroyed or saw heavy damage. Friends in the U.S. gave us more than $35,000 to rebuild. Seven years later you cannot tell a storm ever hit the island. In all it was estimated the storm did $2.5 billion in damage but today the country is back to normal.

As it was in Haiti, the work in Grenada has been blessed beyond words by teams from U.S. churches visiting. I regret that I failed to keep this record but am confident in went into the hundreds. Work teams have come on several occasions to build or repair buildings. Many others have visited to lead VBS programs. Jonathan Parker and his wife, Becky from Gretna, VA have been very effective in setting up a free dental clinic. Others have come to conduct seminars or teach leadership. All have been a great blessing to the work. The church in Grenada continues to grow and be a blessing in this nation.

2003 was a really busy year for us. I made three trips into Grenada covering about eight weeks. I conducted fifteen weeks of revival in the U.S. and preached most of the Lord's days between these. By the time I came to North Danville church in Danville, Va. for a September 22-25 revival I was really exhausted. I was glad it was within driving distance of home since I could rest and sleep in my own bed. I had noticed for a month or so that I felt tired and just couldn't seem to rest. I finished in Danville and went home to rest. I was to leave the next Tuesday for another meeting in Cincinnati, OH but instead ended up at Veterans Hospital in Durham, NC where I underwent triple bypass heart surgery. There were a few glitches in the operation and I had to be taken back to surgery and opened up a second time within twenty four hours. After five days I was released to return home and began the long process of healing. Since I didn't have a heart attack I was counting on bounding back quickly. I had already cancelled meetings in Ohio, North Carolina, and West Virginia so I was anxious to get back to work. After less than a week at home I returned to the hospital with infection in my leg. The doctors treated me and in a couple of days sent me home again. I had spent all of October seeing doctors and being treated but didn't really feel I was doing much better. Discouragement began to set in for the first time since the surgery. I began to wonder if I would ever be able to resume my ministry. I never dreamed I would miss preaching so much. I woke up really sick on November 6 and Patsy called the doctors at Durham. They advised her to bring me back and upon arrival they began treating me for kidney failure. For the first time since surgery it dawned on me that I might very well be finished as a preacher. I remember praying and asking God if he would grant me an extension of life. I would love to see the work in Grenada become fully self supporting. There were other places I wanted to teach and preach if it was His will. The following entries in Patsy's diary says it all.

*Saturday night - Nov. 9*
*While driving home from the hospital at 8:41 PM, I asked God to touch Louis and cause his kidneys to start functioning again. I felt my spirit agreeing with the Holy Spirit that he was being healed. Praise God! Louis is going to be alright. Thank you Lord. In Jesus name. (Life can be awful but God is good.)*

*Tuesday-Nov. 12*
*Thank God. Louis is feeling better. His kidneys are improving. Thank God for answered prayer. We know he is going to recover.*

On the 17th I was able to return home and day by day I became stronger. The nine years since this ordeal have been some of my best years in evangelism. God heard our prayers and granted me the extension I asked for. I can only praise Him for this.

On January 6, 2005 my dear Mother, Dorothy Virginia Craighead Hall slipped quietly out of this life to be with Jesus. She was 97 years of age and still living at home where we had been raised. I am sure the first truth ever taught me in life was taught by Mom. Her kind and loving spirit was always evident in her day to day living. I saw Mom's tenderness when just a young boy. I had placed my pet rabbit under a wooden box in the yard. Not knowing the rabbit was beneath the box, she went to move it and when the rabbit started to run out she put the box down quickly, hitting the rabbit and killing it. She cradled it in her arms and cried. I saw that tenderness each time one of her boys returned to military life after being home. Mom had not an unkind word toward anyone. She could see a bright cloud behind every storm. Once my brother Joe was telling her about a man that had a bad drinking problem. He asked Mom to pray for this man because he was drinking a case of beer every day. Mom quickly said, "Oh, tell him to save those cans. He can get money for them." Mom had a tremendous prayer life and we all counted on her to pray for us as we served the Lord in various ways. She, more than anyone, taught me right from wrong and instilled in me the desire to make something worthwhile of my life. Her love and prayers for me had more influence on me than she could have ever dreamed. Ten of the twelve children she raised are still living and we all miss her every day.

    The years between 2005 and 2008 continued to be busy years with regular trips into Grenada and great numbers of revivals in the U.S. I rejoice to write that not one meeting was cancelled due to sickness and God blessed with many souls added. My notes indicate that VBS teams from Virginia, Florida and Ohio blessed us with their presence during those years. The church in Grenada continues to mature in Christ.

    I returned from Grenada in April of 2009 and preached a revival in West Virginia. From there I came to Mt Olive church in Belhaven, NC for a week of preaching. I was to share the preaching each night with brother Reggie Thomas of Joplin, MO. This was a great pleasure for me to be with this able preacher of the word. Reggie had been preaching much longer than I and had traveled in much of the world with the Gospel. During the week we shared a house on the river and had opportunity to share experiences. Since we both graduated from the same bible college we knew many of the same people and had preached in many of the same places. He asked me if I would consider going to Liberia in West Africa later in the year. They had just come through 14 years of civil war and the opportunities were great for preaching the Gospel there. I told Reggie I would pray about it and give it some serious consideration. In the meantime I needed to find a map and see where Liberia was.

## Toowoomba, Australia- November 18 -December 12, 2008

On November 18, 2008 Patsy and I made a trip "down under" to beautiful Australia. I had been there several years earlier with Jim Newman as he explored the possibility of moving there to serve. On the first trip we had visited with Delroy Brown at Toowoomba and he invited Jim and Becky to come work with him. They accepted the invitation and had moved down the next year.

Now Jim and Becky had moved just out of Toowoomba and started a new work in their home. This was a great move and has grown to several more house churches in this area. I mentioned earlier in the book that Jim is a great student and teacher of the Bible and excels in preparing and making available solid, Bible-centered material.

Patsy taught the women of the church and I taught the men. We did this for about a week and then had the opportunity to travel south to Sidney and take in some of the sights of this beautiful country. The time with our old friends and co-workers in Grenada, Jim and Becky Newman, was a great joy to us. We spent about a week making the trip south and were able to visit some of the other Christians and churches along the way.

While visiting in Sidney we took a tour of the world famous Opera House. One of the things that had long been on my "bucket list" was to sing here, so once we entered the great auditorium I started to quietly sing. I was doing pretty good until Patsy gave me that dirty look like she used to give our kids, so I quit. Maybe it was my selection, "Old McDonald Had a Farm." Anyway, how many other people do you know personally who sang at the Sidney Opera House?

The Newmans are doing a great work in Australia and it was a great pleasure to spend this month with them. We're hoping to be able to visit again in the near future.

Above: Patsy talking with Doug via ham radio from Grenada
Below: Vacation Bible School in St. Georges, Grenada

My sweet mother Dorothy Hall

Patsy's dad Argel McBee

Becky and Jim Newman who started the work in Grenada

## LIBERIA, WEST AFRICA - Oct. 29, 2009

    I had preached in several countries of the world but never in any of the countries on the continent of Africa. I had friends who had lived and served in places like Zambia, Ethiopia, and South Africa, but I had never even visited the continent of Africa. Up to this writing I have made three trips into Liberia with a fourth planned for October 2012. In the three trips, 1,202 have been baptized into Christ. On October 29, 2009 I flew from Raleigh-Durham to NYC where I changed planes and flew to Brussels, Belgium. In Belgium I met with Steve Butler from Kansas, and with Ken, Mark, and Sue from California. After about a five hour wait in Belgium, the five of us boarded the six hour flight to Liberia, West Africa. It was thrilling to finally step foot on African soil. The airport was lacking in facilities and in a run down state. I knew the country was just ending a 14 year civil war but had no idea it would be as bad as it was. It was at least a two hour ride by car from the airport into the city of Monrovia. The effects of the long war could be seen wherever you looked. The road was in great need of repair and the landscape was scarred by years of fighting. People stood by the side of the road with outstretched arms, begging for anything you would give them. I thought as I surveyed the countryside that the poverty was as bad as we saw in Haiti. As we entered the city of Monrovia I was amazed at the war damage. Entire buildings had been blown away and only the shell left standing. Bullet holes could be seen in store fronts and most of the stores were vacant. I would soon learn that this damage was nothing compared to the damage and destruction done to the gentle people who live there.
    We were fortunate to find rooms at the Metropolitan Hotel in the heart of the city. It's a well worn, battle scarred old hotel but it's a safe place with plenty of security. There was no food available but plenty of bottled water and a fairly safe-looking Greek restaurant about two blocks away. For security reasons Steve and I agreed to stay in the same room. Ken and Mark shared a room and Sue was on her on but between the two rooms we had.

Sometime during the night we were awakened with a knock at the door. Ken informed us that Mark was in difficulty and feared that he was suffering a heart attack. I went to his room and observed him. He appeared to me to be having a panic attack, brought on by culture shock. By daylight we had gotten him to the John F. Kennedy Hospital where he was examined and released. Still not feeling well he decided to fly back home to California, so he and Ken left on the evening flight. That would leave only Steve and I to preach. Carol would work with the children at the Orphanage.

Steve and I each teamed with an African evangelist and preached in a different part of Monrovia . I worked with Liberian evangelist Julius Winkler for the first four nights, and in spite of heavy rains that closed some of our roads and soaked us and the crowds, we saw 68 respond to confess Christ and be baptized. Where there was no body of water large enough to immerse, we used children's swimming pools we brought in. If you fill them up and have the candidate sit in the pool you can then immerse them easily. Steve reported 42 baptisms his first four nights.

Here I'm including an entry from my journal for November 2 :

*"Started very early this morning after a really great night's rest. We made our way by car as far as we could toward a village recently contacted. There is a small church of Christ here with about sixty members. From the road we walked to the village about two miles away. The houses are of straw and mud with no grass about them. Living conditions are more primitive than anywhere I have ever witnessed, even in India. Smiling children greeted us with shouts of laughter before we even arrived. The orange tint in the children's hair indicated signs of malnutrition. We sang some happy Christian songs and the sound of singing soon brought in a crowd of one hundred or more. My message was short, perhaps twenty minutes and at the conclusion, five adult women stepped out of the crowd to confess Christ as Lord. We then walked about a quarter mile to a stream of water where one of the men from the church immersed them. From the stream*

the church walked back to the village singing African Christian songs. Oh how God has blessed me to allow me to announce the Gospel on this continent so far from home."

In spite of the rains we continued to conduct street meetings in and around Monrovia each evening. The second half of my preaching was on Bushrod Island with evangelist Eujay. By the end of that week we would see 123 more obey the Gospel. That brought the total for both of us to 238 souls. I rejoiced in that but could not help but wonder what the results would have been with more workers. When brother Julius asked if I would recruit a team to come next year, I said yes and began to think of who I could invite.

The Christians in Liberia have an amazing testimony. When a rebel group backed by the government of Guinea attacked their country in 1989, it would savagely kill and maim the people until 2003. More than 150,000 people would be killed and many thousands displaced. Small children were forced to kill their own people. Anyone born around 1975 and having lived through this period has a story to tell. Every one of our preachers can tell stories of watching family members die. One of our young preachers quietly told me this story as he and I sat drinking coffee:

*"Early one morning as we were eating breakfast we heard gunfire and shouts and realized the rebels were coming through our village. Their practice was to enter a house, steal, rape, and kill and usually set fire to the house as they left. Quite often they would kill everyone in the house. We were Christians and knew we would suffer more abuse than others. Upon seeing them approach our house, my older sister who was sixteen ran outside and willingly gave herself to the soldiers. They brutally raped and abused her. I could hear her weeping but soon the rebels passed on and our house was not entered."*

Mike Foday is one of the strong leaders in the church of Christ in Liberia. As he and I sat at lunch one day, I asked about a scar across his ear and head. He softly told me the story of a rebel soldier who held a rifle on him while another began raping his young daughter. When he jumped to protect her he was shot and forced to watch the ordeal. The daughter had a baby as a result of the rape and is loved dearly by grandpa Mike and being raised in his Christian home.

Many other Christians in Liberia tell of trying to flee to neighboring countries or hiding out in the bush as long as they could. I'm sometimes embarrassed to realize that while all of this was happening in this West African country from 1989 until 2003, like most Americans I was going about my business and hardly noticing it in the news. I asked one of our young preachers what brought the war to an end and he replied, "250 U.S. Marines."

## Liberia, West Africa- October 21, 2010

After spending several weeks in this war-torn country I determined it would be a safe place for Patsy so when I returned the next year she was with me. We had a few problems getting there. We missed our flight in New York and arrived a day after the rest of the team had come in. At baggage claim we learned out suitcases had not made it and it would be several days before they finally did arrive. The total number on our Gospel team numbered fourteen. Two were from Ivory Coast, one from Haiti and eleven from the U.S. A. These consisted of four women and ten men. The women would sing and teach other women as well as work at the orphanage. The ten men would each team with a Liberian evangelist and we would go out for personal evangelism in the morning and conduct Gospel meetings each night. This gave us ten different meetings going on simultaneously each night in all different parts of the city. We arrived on Monday and our clothes didn't reach us until Thursday, but different team members shared clothing with us so we made out fine until our suitcases arrived. When I was telling about this later in one of the churches in North Carolina, I said, "We were in Africa for four days without clothes." When the laughter subsided I explained what I meant by that.

These were extremely busy days. We began each morning with breakfast and devotions with the entire team at 7 AM. During this time we would each give a report of our meetings the night before and share any particular problem we might be having or any special prayer requests. By 11 AM we met with our Liberian evangelist and went out for visitation. We tried to return by 3:30 PM and rest until about 6 PM when we would go out again for preaching services. Most of us would return by 10 PM, eat a snack, and be in bed before midnight. My goal had been to carry in or purchase while there at least one thousand Bibles and Patsy and I were praying that we would see one thousand souls obey the Gospel. With what we had been given by Pine Grove church in West Virginia and County Line church at Axton, Virginia, we had the Bibles and at the conclusion of our meetings we had witnessed nine hundred and thirty baptized into Christ. It was by far the greatest Gospel preaching campaign I had ever been in. Immediately after each baptism the new convert was given a Bible and enrolled in a six week new member class. Throughout the day and often at night, Patsy would be in a village church teaching the women or children or both.

I have worked with teams from many places in America and elsewhere but cannot honestly say I have ever witnessed a team work together with such love and unity. Mark and Janet Layman are an older couple from the Kiamichi Mountains of Oklahoma and such a joy to be around. Reggie Thomas is an 83 year old preacher who has traveled the world with the Gospel. I'm amazed at his boundless energy and great vision. The smile never leaves his face. The African Christians call him "Daddy." Reggie lives in Joplin, MO. Tom Mulinex is a Texas preacher with a love for statistics. He established churches in Ivory Coast and is full of faith. Dr. Blythe Robinson is a brilliant man of God. He's worked in many countries of the world and is very effective among Muslims. A fearless preacher of the word, Blythe has a dry wit about him and is ready and willing to go anywhere on earth with the Gospel. I heard no complaining from any team member and everyone was willing to do whatever they were asked to do the entire time.

With her permission, here I insert a few lines from Patsy's daily diary during this trip.

*"We are staying at the Metropolitan Hotel. We have a bathroom, a bed, and a mouse........Tonight Louis spoke to a small boy about three and the little boy began to cry. His Mother said Louis was the first white man he had ever seen. Louis said, "don't worry about it, the first time I saw a black man I cried and ran and hid under the bed"..........We went to a place tonight called, "Thinkers Village." Six were baptized into Christ..........Louis bought $500 worth of Bibles today. These will be given out at Thinkers Village............Tonight I took the video camera down to the street to take some pictures. Two guards stopped me and told me not to*

*go outside. One of them said, "There are bad boys out there who will take your camera". I stood in the doorway and filmed.....In five nights we have baptized 500 people......Last night Louis preached about the prodigal son. He used two small boys out of the audience and acted out the scripture. Louis was the Father and when the young son returned home Louis ran and hugged him. The huge audience was so moved they applauded. Eight young Muslim men were baptized into Christ........ God is so good to allow us to come to Liberia and meet these poor but wonderful people."*

## Svishtov, Bulgaria Eastern Europe - May 2011

After Patsy finished a Ladies Retreat in Grundy, VA and I preached at Grundy church of Christ, we returned home to prepare for a first time trip to Bulgaria in Eastern Europe. Several months before, Barbara Barger of Tulsa, OK had called Patsy and invited her to make a trip with her to Bulgaria to teach women and children in this former Communist country. In the same phone conservation she asked if I could also go since they would be alone. She was not sure what opportunities there would be for me but had been promised I could preach in the small church there and witness wherever this was possible. I decided this was an open door and so on May 24 we flew to Germany where we met Barbara and continued on to Sofia, Bulgaria. Sofia is the capitol and a bustling city of several million with no New Testament church. We were met there by Elena Fileva where we traveled by car the 150 miles North to Svishtov on the Danube river. The scenery across Bulgaria was beautiful but the buildings were old, drab, and dreary, typical Russian architecture. The people we saw along the way seemed sad and tired. We would learn while here that Bulgarians seldom smile and being without Christ they have little to smile about or hope in. Bulgaria allied with Germany during World War 2 and so suffered defeat during that time, and in 1946 became a Communist country. The citizens of Bulgaria lived hard under Communism. When Communism crumbled in 1990 Bulgaria became a democracy for the first time but in the words of the people their country is run by the Mafia. They have continued to suffer persecution as before.

One of the first things I noticed after arriving in Svishtov was how lacking in joy everyone seemed to be. I love to laugh but no one much ever seemed to laugh here. When you walked on the street and approached people no one's eyes met yours. They looked away or down. It began to dawn on me that they had learned not to trust anyone. If I laughed and tried to joke with someone in a restaurant or on the street, I had a hidden motive for it. Communicating was harder than anywhere I had ever been. Lying and stealing was accepted since they had learned to do this under Communism. One man told us the true story of a man who stood up in church and testified, "I want to give God thanks. I stole some wood the other night and didn't get caught."

Elena Fileva was born in Macedonia in 1975. While a student in a Christian College she met and married her husband. They became the parents of two daughters and a son. Life was a struggle for them financially and they moved around a good bit. In time he began to physically abuse her, putting her in the hospital on two occasions. He vowed he would kill her if she ever left him. In 2007 she realized she had to escape from this abuse and so she took the children and ran for her life. She told me, "I arrived in Svishtov with three small children and one small suitcase." A friend whom she had met at a Christian camp years before took her in and hid her in the attic of her house. At last she was safe, or so she thought. Without warning her husband showed up in town, came to the house and demanded she and the children come with him. He admitted to beating her and gave as his reason, "She wouldn't obey me." When I asked her why she hadn't called the police she replied, "It would have done no good. They don't care about this." At this time a meeting took place that would free Elena and the children from this abuse forever. A friend of mine whom I shall leave nameless met with Elena's husband and warned him to leave town and never bother her again. He repeated his claim that she was his wife and he could do whatever he liked with her. He was not leaving town without her. My friend then warned him, "I have close friends in the Mafia. If you persist in bothering her, you will disappear from this earth." He left immediately and has never bothered her again. I asked him if he really knew Mafia people and he replied, "Absolutely. There are swamps outside this town where a person could be taken and never heard from again."

Elena and the children now have their own small apartment and though life is a daily struggle, they are free and happy in Christ. Patsy and I count her as a close friend. She is a beautiful woman both inside and out and we've come to love her like a daughter. We're glad that our mission has been able to assist her and the children from time to time. Patsy has sent clothing and needed funds to help her during this past hard winter when the temperature dropped to -29°F and many died. She has been our link to the work in Svishtov just as Lydia was to Paul in Macedonia.

Patsy was kept much busier than I with Bible lessons with the women every day. These were held in the homes and were geared to offer encouragement as well as solid Christian doctrine. I preached on the Lord's day in the small store front building where the "Good News" church meets. They baptize believers in the Danube river, call themselves "Christians," but take the Lord's supper only once each month. I studied this with the young minister but as of now have not convinced him this is really why the early Christians met on the Lord's day. We took the Lord's supper in Elena's apartment on Sunday afternoon. One of my most interesting teaching sessions was with a man named Ivan. He had been a soldier in the Russian army and had fought in Afghanistan. Ivan didn't believe in God but his wife, Savetilina had recently become a Christian and Patsy was teaching her. Ivan runs a fishing tackle shop and was delighted to meet someone who enjoyed fishing as he did. We each shared some "fish stories." He roared with laughter when I told him that in America we could always tell if a fisherman was lying.... his lips would be moving.

My study with Ivan on Saturday afternoon had to do with the resurrection of Christ. He had requested we study this. I used the approach I have used on many occasions when teaching this, "What happened to the body of Jesus?" He agreed the friends or enemies of Christ could not or would not have stolen the body. I waited for him to give the only other explanation, "He arose from the dead." and he said it. He was at worship the next morning and sat through my message entitled, "Jesus", but he failed to respond. The last thing I said to Ivan before leaving his country was, "I'm going to be praying you will give your life to Christ."

While in Svishtov I walked one day down to the beautiful Danube river. As I stood on the bank and looked across the river about a quarter mile away, I suddenly realized I was looking at the town of Zimnicea in Romania. This is where minister Richard Wurmbrand was arrested by the Communists and spent fourteen and a half years in prison, more than two years of this in solitary confinement underground. When he was finally released the doctors were amazed to learn from x-rays that almost every bone in his body had been broken from constant beatings during these years. He had bouts with Tuberculous and suffered from malnutrition the entire time. He emerged from prison anything but bitter. His captors were puzzled at his joy. He counted it one of his greatest opportunities to be used of God and to minister to those who were suffering and dying all around him. He had been scheduled to die many times but God had kept him alive for some reason. He ministered to thousands and watched most of them die during these fourteen and one half years. When he was released from prison in 1964 he wrote:

*"The prison years did not seem too long for me, for I discovered, alone in my cell, that beyond belief and love there is a delight in God: a deep and extraordinary ecstasy of happiness that is like nothing in this world. And when I came out of jail I was like someone who comes down from a mountaintop where he has seen for miles around the peace and beauty of the countryside, and now returns to the plain."* (In God's Underground)

I only pray if I ever get into a situation like that in my efforts around this world that I will have the faith and trust to respond in that fashion. As I looked across the river I hoped that I would have the opportunity to preach Christ in Romania one day.

The Christians in Bulgaria are looked upon with suspicion and considered a cult. In recent years police have stood by and done nothing as Christian groups were attacked by anti-Christian groups. Good jobs and promotions are often denied those who profess faith in Christ. We were asked to speak to a high school English class in a public school but told not to mention God or the Bible. To our delight we learned the class had just read one of C.S.

Lewis' books, "The Lion, The Witch, and the Wardrobe." The students asked us to help them write their report on the book. Patsy quizzed the class on what each of these meant and was able to show the difference between God and Satan. She explained that the Lion represented Christ and his sacrifice for us, while the Witch represented Satan. I was proud of her ability to use this opportunity as a way to present Christ. The teacher later told us he had not heard one negative report of our visit but many favorable things.

We left our dear friends in Bulgaria with a lump in our throats and tears in our eyes but with the knowledge that if did not see them again in this life we would see them again when we all reached our heavenly home.

## Grenada, West Indies-Jan.2 2011

We returned to Grenada, West Indies on January 2 and were joined the next day by our old friends, Jim and Becky Newman of Australia. What a happy two weeks this would be with them. Jim and I would be teaching each evening and the church had asked him to preach on the Lord's day. On January 9 Jean Anglais church would celebrate its 25th year with more than one hundred in attendance. Jim and Becky had planted this church so it was fitting they could come back for this special day. During that week I had the joy of baptizing Nicholas Hosten into Christ. This church was now a self supporting, self governing, and self propagating church. We all had reason to rejoice over how God has blessed on the island of Grenada. Patsy and I continue to work with the church here on the "Isle of Spice."

## Liberia, West Africa -October 28, 2011

Our third trip into Liberia took place on October 28 with the usual flight from New York to Belgium to Ivory Coast and finally into Monrovia, Liberia. We stayed at the Metropolitan Hotel again. We could no doubt find better accommodations for the same price but this hotel is centrally located and a secure place to stay. Our team consisted of six: two from Michigan, one from Indiana, one from Texas and two of us from Virginia. We arrived the night of the 29th and began preaching and teaching the next day. Two of my nieces, Hope Mullins, and Kimberly Nance and Kimberly's daughter Beth had made 172 pillow case dresses to be given to the children of Africa, and these were a tremendous blessing wherever we went. I preached the first week in a village on Bushrod Island called "Chicken Soup." It was primitive and difficult to get to because the rain produced deep ruts in the road. They had constructed a speaker's stand from scraps of lumber. It was about fifteen feet off the ground and pretty shaky. It reminded me of some deer stands I have tried to hunt from. This was the rainy season and after the boards were soaked with rain they were slick.

I remember thinking that all I needed was to fall off the platform and break a leg. I don't know how Patsy would have ever gotten me back home. The next night I stood on the ground to preach. When we met for breakfast the next morning I announced, "Last night we baptized ten in Chicken Soup." The team all got a laugh out of this. I continued to preach here each night for a week and rejoiced to see 29 obey the Gospel. The second week I preached each night about an hour out of town in a place called VOA. I was curious as to how the area got its name and learned that several years ago Voice of America had a large broadcast tower here. The crusade site was ideally situated at the intersection of two main roads where many people traveled. Our largest crowds attended here, with as many as seven hundred on several nights. God gave us 45 baptisms during this second week.

The young African evangelist I was working with at VOA had tremendous energy and enthusiasm. Well educated, he teaches part time in a college in Monrovia but is working hard to build up the church of Christ at VOA. He and I would visit door to door in the village each day and conduct services in the evening. One night he told a large crowd before I preached, *"This old man amazes me! He's been out walking all day. He's an old man and should be somewhere lying down, but here he is ready to preach to us."* We had a big laugh out of this and still do. Sometimes when Patsy asks me to do some chore around the house, I remind her I'm an old man and should be somewhere lying down, but she doesn't buy it.

One of the Deacons of the church latched on to me the minute we arrived there. He could not do enough for me. He carried my Bible and camera and anything else I might be carrying. He made sure to shine the flashlight at my feet so I wouldn't stumble over anything. His service to me was almost to the point of being embarrassing. It was obvious from his clothing that he was a poor man. He was small of stature so I couldn't share my clothes with him. Wanting to show my appreciation, on the last night before services began, I very discreetly placed a fairly large piece of money in his hand. He put in his pocket, smiled and thanked me. Later in the service when the offering basket was brought out, he took the gift I had given him and put it in the basket. We had planned to be out of Liberia before November 8 when the National election would take place. We knew there would be a lot of protesting and action in the streets and we wished to avoid this. Several people died during demonstrations but the election took place as scheduled and President Ellen Sirleaf was elected for another term. We learned years ago that a third world country is not a good place to be on election day.

We conducted several work projects on this trip. Two fish ponds were constructed and stocked with Talapia fish. In six months they will be big enough to market. A cement block machine was purchased so a church could make its own blocks for construction but also to sell. Our plans are to present more and more ways for Christians to make a living and become self sufficient in these third world countries.

When the team left Liberia on November 6 we rejoiced that 242 persons had confessed the name of Christ and obeyed him in baptism. We have found Liberia a great place to work and are making plans to return there in October 2012.

## North Africa -March 1-12, 2012

Sometime in late 2011 two dear friends of mine, Beth and William Sawyer, asked me to accompany them on a trip to a country in North Africa. I gladly jumped at the chance to go. The workers in this country asked us not to identify it by name, nor to give their names since missionary work is frowned on in this country. They were going there to encourage a friend. We would spend our time here in prayer and would witness whenever the opportunity presented itself. This country was more than 90% Muslim. We traveled from north to south and never saw one church building or cross anywhere. There are no religious broadcasts nor can you purchase a Bible in any bookstore in the entire country. Some four hundred Christians are known to live here. I was greatly moved by how much they loved the Lord and the price they are willing to pay in order to be faithful.

As is the case in many countries in Africa, political unrest, protests, and uprisings are almost a daily occurrence in this country. One day as we were traveling in the southern part of the country we suddenly came to a roadblock. The road had been completely closed by huge stones and some ten or twelve young men stood there. We were blessed to have a young Christian convert with us who spoke Arabic. She explained to them that we were visitors and had nothing in their fight with their government. They still refused to allow us to pass and now would not even allow us to turn around and go back the other way. I'll never forget the grave look on her face when she quietly and calmly explained, "They say if you move the car one inch they will stone us."

We sat in the car for what seemed like hours but it was probably not more than five or ten minutes. During that time the five of us prayed that God would not only protect us but that we could somehow witness to this nation of people who did not know Him. Finally one of the young men approached the car and said they had decided to allow us to pass. Five minutes up the road I called Patsy in America. She was surprised to hear from me and exclaimed, "I've just now finished praying for you." I'm convinced that we often underestimate the power and effectiveness of prayer. It made me wonder how many times we have been spared from some great harm or untimely death because someone back home was praying for us. I can only praise God for the great numbers of you who have been prayer warriors for us.

## OTHER GREAT BLESSINGS

In the past thirty years while we have been busy traveling this world with the Gospel, God has been blessing us with grandchildren. Presently we have eight grandchildren, one great grandson, and two great grandchildren due in September. Lynn is the oldest and married to David White. They have one son, Joshua. Lynn is the daughter of Tammy and Greg Hand. Robert is a fireman in Raleigh, NC and married to Kate Rokes. They are expecting their first child in September. Robert is also Tammy and Greg's son. Matthew is married to Megan Brooks and is a K-9 Virginia State trooper. They are expecting their first child in September. He too is a son of Tammy and Greg. Tiffany is the daughter of Doug and Bonnie and teaches school in Raleigh, N.C. She is married to Jeffery Webb who attends North Carolina State University. Christopher is the son of Doug and Bonnie and is married to Beth Evans. They live in Buffalo, NY where Chris works as minister in a new church plant. Jake is a $2^{nd}$ Lt. in the Marine Corps and stationed at Quantico, VA. Luke is a Lance Corporal in the Marine Corps and majoring in Criminal Justice in college. Emily is a sophomore at the University of North Carolina in Greensboro where she is majoring in pre-law. Jake, Luke, and Emily are the children of our daughter, Brenda and her husband, Tommy Haynes. Each one has filled our hearts with thanksgiving. All are Christian and actively serving our great God.

About twelve years ago Patsy and I placed our membership with the County Line Christian church near Axton, Va. I had been acquainted with this fine congregation since early in my ministry and had preached a number of revivals here in the past. Though we are gone a good bit of the time, it's wonderful to have such a loving church family. They have truly opened their arms and hearts to us, supporting our mission work in every way with finances, well wishes and especially prayer support. So many wonderful friendships have been made that I would hardly know where to begin to describe them. On fairly frequent occasions I am asked to preach, teach, or do a mission presentation. Their response is always one of appreciation and enthusiasm. Though the church building is almost an hour's drive from our home, it is well worth the drive to be a part of such a loving fellowship. The church is blessed to have a fine group of elders and teachers and is served by two well qualified ministers in Dean Ashby and Tim Maness. Friendships have been made among the members of this church that will follow us into eternity.

## WHAT'S NEXT IN MINISTRY FOR US?

Today is May 19, 2012. I am 76 years old. I entertain no thoughts of retiring or doing anything else other than what I have been doing for the past 54 years. My calendar for the remainder of the year is filled with revivals and mission meetings. I do not know what God's calendar says about my future. We are scheduled to teach in Grenada in July and will be returning to West Africa in late October. Other trips abroad are pending. I thank God for the health and strength He has supplied to enable us to do what we've done.

My all-time favorite preacher of the Gospel was Knowles Shaw. He was born in Butler County Ohio in 1834 and only preached about 19 years before he was killed in a train wreck in Texas. During his short ministry he baptized more than 20,000 souls into Christ. The last words he spoke on this earth were seconds before the train wrecked and took his life. He told a friend, "Oh! It is a grand thing to rally the people to the cross." This great traveling evangelist wrote that beautiful song, "Bringing in the sheaves." One verse in that song says:

> Sowing in the sunshine. Sowing in the shadows;
> Fearing neither clouds or winter's chilling breeze.
> By and by the harvest and the labor ended
> We shall come rejoicing bringing in the sheaves.

Someday the great Lord of the harvest will call us home. Oh! How I pray I will hear Him say, "Well done good and faithful servant. Enter into the joy of the Lord." My ministry has been full of excitement and joy and I have rejoiced to see what great things God was doing. No greater blessing could have ever been given to me like the JOY OF THE HARVEST. It could have never happened without His leading and without the friendship and partnership of multitudes of you.

-END-

## PATSY'S PAGE

Louis has concluded his book but not his ministry. I feel I must say something about his life as a minister of the gospel. I have been with him for the past 53 years and have witnessed and shared in the joys and the hardships of his life. The joys of seeing people come to Christ. The sadness over others who rejected Him. Whatever the outcome Louis always found great joy in preaching Christ. I have been by his side in Haiti, Grenada, Bulgaria, Liberia and in many hundreds of meetings across America. Nothing brought us more happiness than seeing eternal souls respond to our Savior.

There are so many things in our long ministry that have made life so wonderful and fulfilling. Outside of the Lord and salvation, I count our children, Doug, Tammy and Brenda as our greatest blessings. Oh! The stories I could tell about them!

Our eight grandchildren are also tremendous blessings from God. The fact that they know the Lord and are serving Him has also filled us with thanksgiving. Now we have a great grandson and two more will be born in September. As you read this there may be more. [Ed. Note: yes, one more, due February 2012!]

We have met people around this world who have become our dearest friends. Children in foreign lands have become our children and grandchildren. We have great numbers of them in the West Indies, Europe and Africa. What a joy it will be to see these dear people in Heaven when we meet our Lord. As we grown older we long more for heaven and our new bodies, where there will be no more sorrow and only the sunshine of our Lord Jesus Christ.

There are so many stories we could share that this book would never end. Louis has shared quite a few but others have been forgotten until something happens that bring them to mind again.

I believe God has a plan for our lives. It's up to us if we follow that plan or not. My dear friend, Carolyn Walker, brought me to the Lord. I am so glad I followed her example and met Christ. I met Louis at Cincinnati Christian University. I truly believe that it was God's plan for us to marry and for me to be by his side in this ministry. We will never know the true impact our lives have had in this world until we reach Heaven. What wonderful words, "Well done good and faithful servant." I pray we will hear those words one day.

Whenever we hear of a need anywhere in the world, Louis will say, "Let's go there and help them." We flew to Alaska and saw a great need for preachers. Louis thought we could go there. He could buy another plane and resume his flying. He could hunt and fish and stay busy preaching and evangelizing. It would be wonderful. I grew up in West Virginia and Ohio and endured winters that were too cold for me back then. I don't think I could survive even one below zero, let alone forty below. As he talked about it, he asked, "What do you think you would miss most if we moved to Alaska?" I answered, "You." Needless to say, though we moved some, we didn't move to Alaska.

I was born in West Virginia and have many cousins still living there. My sister, Billie and her family live in Ohio. My brother, Jerry and sister, Betty are deceased but their families still live fairly close by in Ohio. I visit my sister once or twice a year and it's always great fun to talk about old times. Like me, she is a gad-about. When we're together we always have to go somewhere, even if it's only Walmart.

I am proud of my family and love them dearly. God has given us a really large and loving family in the church. I have had a great life serving with Louis in this ministry. God has provided our every need and opened doors we never dreamed could open. We often talk about times we were in real danger in foreign countries and took some foolish chances. We were in Haiti when two governments were overthrown and the violence was severe. He brought us out safe and sound without a scratch.

We're both moving much slower than we once did, but still active in His harvest and praying we can continue on until He calls us home. I hope you enjoyed Louis' book about his interesting life and our victorious ministry.

- Patsy McBee Hall

## A FUNNY THING HAPPENED AT CHURCH

I have always enjoyed laughing and often use humor in my preaching and teaching. What follows are a few of the things I've heard and witnessed that made me laugh. They prove that some of the funniest things happen either at church or with church people.

The minister at my home church back in the late 50's was making announcements and with his Mississippi drawl he said, "Don't forget that next Sunday will be Building Sun Funday."

I was announcing our revival in Ohio and encouraging people to bring their neighbor. I said, "I don't want to see one car pull into this parking lot with no one in it."

My dear friend, Ben James was preaching about Noah and the great flood. He said, "The animals came into the Ark two by two.... the Hippopotamus and the Kangaroo."

We had a new Deacon who had never prayed in public and when an elder called on him to give thanks for the offering, he prayed, "Lord, watch these men as they go around taking up the money."

Sherma was getting her children ready for church in Grenada when she noticed Nick had his shoes on the wrong feet. She said, "Nick, you have your shoes on the wrong feet." He began to cry and said, "No mama, These are *my* feet."

A Georgia preacher who was accustomed to baptizing a lot of people was marrying a young couple and at the conclusion of the ceremony he said, "I pronounce you husband and wife in the name of the Father, Son and Holy Spirit.... for the forgiveness of your sins and gift of the Holy Spirit."

During a prayer circle in Tennessee one night, one of the men prayed, "And Lord, please forgive us for our falling shorts."

During the singing of "Love Lifted Me" one of my friends listened closely and noted his young brother was singing, "Love Lipton tea."

A classmate of mine stood up to preach in Ohio one Sunday night and discovered his notes were missing from his Bible. He paused a moment and said to the church, "You'll have to give me a minute to collect my thoughts." After a second or two he said, "To be honest, I have no thoughts to collect."

A well known church of Christ preacher got on the elevator on the first floor of a hospital and pushed the button for the second floor. When the door opened he stepped off and said to the full elevator, "Folks, when I die, this is the direction I want to go." Someone on the elevator said, "Not me!" He then noticed they were in the basement.

Several years ago I was flying from Hong Kong to Thailand. I got out my Bible and a lady sitting next to me said, "I don't believe the Bible. I don't even believe there is a God." I replied, "Is that right?" I went back to my reading and in a short time we ran into a storm with really rough air. The huge 747 was dropping and bouncing wildly. In a few minutes the lady next to me said, "Pray, Reverend!" I answered, "To whom?"

A young minister was waxing quite eloquent in a message about Abraham and Lot. He meant to quote the scripture from Genesis 13:12. "Abraham lived in the land of Canaan while Lot lived among the cities of the plain and pitched his tents toward Sodom." When quoting it, he said "Lot pinched his tit toward Sodom."

In a revival one hot August in Edon, Ohio a small boy began to cry. I raised my volume to get above him and the baby did likewise. Finally the young mother got up and was taking the baby out. Like a fool I asked the mother not to take the baby out and assured her he was not bothering me. As she went through the door with the small child on her hip, she called back, "You sure are bothering him."

My brother Russell was in the middle of a great message about Moses when he said, "Down in his heart Moses knew he was not Pharaoh's daughter."

What if we all tried to do it when the preacher said, "Turn over in your Bibles..."

Did you ever smile when the preacher started a sentence with, "If you are here today..."

In several of my ministries it was my job to prepare the weekly bulletin. One of the elders called and told me to be sure and announce the Board meeting in this week's bulletin. I never convinced him it was a typographical error when I printed, "There will be a meeting of the BORED after services today."

I once saw in a bulletin this announcement, "For those of you who have children and don't know it, we have a nursery in the basement."

My friend and brother Rodney Thomas was conducting his first wedding in Grenada, West Indies and was a little nervous about it. I was going over the ceremony with him and suggested that he omit the line, "If anyone can show cause why these may not be joined together." He decided to go with it anyway and when he came to that part he boldly proclaimed, "If anyone can show just cause why these may not be joined together, let him now speak or hereafter forever hold his peace." He then paused for a few seconds, lifted his hands and said, "No one?"

During a morning service in Grenada a parrot flew into an open window and perched on a bench in back. The parrot began making a squawking noise and brother Rodney stopped his message and said to Lystra, "Pick up your son and stop him from making that noise with his shoes." (He had not seen the parrot.) Lystra said, "Rodney, that's not my son. It's the parrot." Rodney paused a minute and said, "I rebuke that parrot in the name of the Lord." The entire church roared with laughter when the parrot flew back out the window.

During my morning message in Grenada suddenly more than half the audience got up and ran out of the building. I stopped and waited and could see them in the church yard, looking up. In a short time they returned and took their seats. I then remembered and asked, "Maria, did you see the Concord?" She smiled and replied, "No, brother Hall. Too cloudy."

I attended the funeral of a man I knew in Grenada who weighed at least three hundred pounds. When the preacher began his funeral message he said, "Rudy was a winner!" Many "amens" went up so he repeated it, "Rudy was a winner!" He then said, "At school years ago when we played tug of war, everyone wanted him on their side."

I read in a church bulletin in Virginia, "The new loudspeaker system just installed was given by brother _____ in memory of his late wife."

After I preached a funeral in High Point, NC the body was taken out into the country for the burial at a small family cemetery. We approached the tent and when the pallbearers placed the casket over the grave there was quite a bit of excitement as we heard scratching and muffled sounds coming forth. The funeral director had them move the casket and rescued a small dog that had fallen into the grave.

This announcement appeared in a church bulletin, "All those who enjoy sinning are asked to join the choir."

A church in the Martinsville Virginia area was between preachers and one of the leaders called to see if I was available to preach a few Sunday's until they got a preacher. When services began on Sunday he made the following announcement, "We welcome Lou Hall today. He has agreed to preach for us until we get a real preacher."

My youngest brother Joe is a great preacher in his own right. After hearing me preach one night he said, "Good job, Louis. I think I could take that and make something out of it."